14.00

# Community Mental Health Legislation

# Community Mental Health Legislation

**The Formative Process**

**Henry A. Foley**
National Institute of Mental
Health

**Lexington Books**
D. C. Heath and Company
Lexington, Massachusetts
Toronto          London

**Library of Congress Cataloging in Publication Data**

Foley, Henry A.
    Community mental health legislation.

    Bibliography: p.
    Includes index.
    1. Mental health laws—United States—History.   2. Community
mental health services—United States.   I. Title. [DNLM: 1. Com-
munity mental health services—U.S.—Legislation.   2. Politics—
U.S. WM30 F663c]
KF3828.F64      344′.73′044      75-189
ISBN 0-669-99374-3

Published simultaneously in Canada

Printed in the United States of America

International Standard Book Number: 0-669-99374-3

Library of Congress Catalog Card Number: 75-189

# Contents

# List of Tables

# Foreword

## The Political Genesis of the Community Health Centers Act

Some readers may be surprised by the argument of this book. Dr. Foley shows how federal officials identified an important problem, promoted the research necessary for a solution, attracted a coalition united in its goals and successful in its lobbying, and, finally, administered the resulting program in a manner faithful to the letter and spirit of the legislation and to the intent of the authors. In short, his unconventional thesis is that the federal government is capable of action that is rational, purposive, and nonincremental.

Dr. Foley's analysis contrasts with the conventional view that policy making in American government is incremental, distributive, and radically pluralistic. According to this view, government action issues typically from a process of bargaining among a set of individuals and groups with no common goal. Policy resulting from such a process is distributive in the sense that so far as the wishes of its various supporters are concerned, each of its components is separable from the others and satisfies the interests of any member of the coalition independently of the other components. Thus, in the classic pork-barrel appropriation, if some particular road, bridge, harbor improvement, or other public work provided for in the bill happened to be the only item that was carried out, the interests seeking this benefit would be as fully satisfied as if all provisions in the bill had been implemented. Complex actions of domestic regulation or foreign policy can also be composite; each of the different groups supporting the various elements in the policy aim at and contribute only one element among many. The essence is that in the intentions of the actors the component parts of the action or policy are connected with one another only by the political fact that the efforts of all members of the coalition are necessary for enactment.

In other words, the outcome of this process of adjustment issues from no comprehensive plan or unifying theory. Individual members of the coalition have goals that are more or less broad or narrow. Given the nature of the process, however, the goal of no single member can anticipate the total outcome, but can constitute only an increment toward its realization. The term *incremental* means "by relatively small steps." In relation to the total outcome, each component effort is one small step toward a composite result that no one intends or foresees. In this sense, policy making by adjustment is inherently incrementalist.

Although incremental and unintended, a policy so formed may do a better job of taking into account the various interests involved than would a rigid or uninformed attempt to plan comprehensively. That is what much of the controversy is about: Which model—the purposive or the adjustive—is more likely to produce rational action? Writers on this question tend to take sides. I hope it does not sound Pollyannish to suggest that each type of decision making can produce rationality or irrationality, and that a task of the political scientist is to try to identify the conditions under which each result is likely to ensue. Clearly, neither approach is a royal road to rational government. The failure of uncontrolled atomism to provide necessary collective goods can be as destructive as a rigid ideological reliance on theory to enforce control.

Although discussion of the two models can get very technical and has generated some formidable jargon, the issues raised lead into familiar and fundamental questions of political science and philosophy. Students of American democracy have frequently been concerned to show that our system does—or should—operate according to one or the other model. I recall first having my eyes opened to the possibilities of the adjustive model when in 1940, as a graduate student, I read E. P. Herring's just published *Politics of Democracy*. In that original and perceptive work Herring laid bare the far-ranging pluralism of American politics and, against this background, appraised the merits of a pervasive mode of action that he termed "adjustment." In those same years when economic collapse at home was being superseded by a far more deadly menace from abroad, other observers took a very different tack, arguing that the demands of the times could be met only by a more purposive and consciously coordinated mode of governance. A contemporary exposition of this view was Schattschneider's *Party Government* (1942). It became a classic in the ensuing controversy over "a more responsible two-party system," in which the purposive and the adjustive models, under various names, were compared, examined, illustrated, defended, attacked, used, and abused by scholars and advocates.

The controversy over party government itself had roots in a further past, stretching back to Woodrow Wilson's dolorous judgment on the dispersion of power in the American system. "Nobody stands sponsor for the policy of the government," he wrote in 1885, in *Congressional Government*. "A dozen men originate it; a dozen compromises twist and alter it; a dozen offices whose names are scarcely known outside of Washington put it into execution." And this view in turn consciously echoed Walter Bagehot's depreciatory comparison between the English system "framed on the principle of choosing a single sovereign authority, and making it good" and the American, based on "the principle of having many sovereign authorities, and hoping that their multitude may atone for their inferiority."

The history of political philosophy presents other exemplars of these two contrasting approaches to government. In the English tradition Burke is surely the outstanding critic of ideological reliance on theory and advocate of gradualism and piecemeal reform, while his younger contemporary, Jeremy Bentham, exudes confidence in the ability of human intelligence to use government to identify problems and impose comprehensive solutions. I will not try to trace any further the lineage of the two models. It must go back a long way, since it manifests one aspect of the deep-seated division of perspective on human affairs between rationalists and irrationalists.

In the past few years there has been a good deal of discussion of the purposive and adjustive models of government action. No single account has come to be accepted as definitive, but surely one of the most lucid and useful analyses is that of Charles Lindblom, who elaborates his conception of the two models under the titles of "mutual partisan adjustment" and "conscious central decision-making." Dr. Foley has used Professor Lindblom's conception as his main analytic tool. Needless to say, in this case study of an actual event, he does not find a pure example of either model. Still, the process he describes resembles the purposive more than the adjustive model. Characterizing that process as "oligopolistic partisan mutual adjustment," he writes:

> The CMHC policy resulted from a process of decision making among allied partisans. Critical political actors made policy according to a process that necessitated explicit agreements and goals. The Community Mental Health Centers Act did not evolve out of a series of marginal moves and uncoordinated decisions that necessitated only vague agreement on broad goals. Rather, the mental health oligopoly provided a public policy responsive to technical knowledge and congressional sentiment.

As I read his analysis, its central theme is the power of theory to initiate, coordinate, and effectuate government action. His story is a classic instance of the great contemporary role of science in public policy. The narrative has not merely a purposive, but indeed something of a conspiratorial thrust. Its central figure is Dr. Robert Felix, who from his early days as a resident was committed to abolishing the state mental hospital in favor of some form of community care. But the compassion of Dr. Felix and his associates would have been ineffectual without the progress of medical knowledge, in particular the advances in chemotherapy in Europe and the further development of the medical technology of community care promoted by Felix and his fellow conspirators in the National Institute of Mental Health. The real hero was impersonal: the advance of science.

It was this new knowledge that provided the basis for the coalition that emerged to mobilize support for the act. This knowledge gave the various individuals and groups in the coalition what Foley terms a "common general goal." Within the terms set by this goal, differences of interest and understanding arose and were bargained out. Within its boundaries the initiative shifted among the main elements: the bureaucratic, the congressional, and the pressure groups. But the coordinating force among them was a complex common purpose arising out of a background of science and technology. The main factor—the principal independent variable—responsible for this quite fundamental reform was not new sentiments or new interests or new values, but new knowledge.

**Samuel H. Beer**
Eaton Professor of the Science of Government
Harvard University
January 1975

# Preface

This book represents the first extensive political analysis of the passage of the Community Mental Health Centers Act of 1963 and 1965. In explaining the political factors related to the origins of the legislation, I have described the political history of the modern mental health movement (1940-70). Historians have left this subject almost entirely unexplored. My description is based on research into published and unpublished records of the National Institute of Mental Health and of professional lobbies and taped interviews with the key political actors. Four central questions guided my examination of these resources:

1. Why did the federal government become increasingly involved in the delivery of services to the mentally ill?

2. From what organizational context and pressures did the decision emerge?

3. Was the decision a result of central decision making or partisans bargaining among themselves?

4. What kinds of lobbying, mobilizing, and bargaining arrangements among which players yielded the critical decision that resulted in a national community mental health program?

The first six chapters constitute a case study of CMHC politics, while chapter 7 describes the conceptual significance of the CMHC case. Chapter 1 describes the centralization of the developing mental health establishment within the National Institute of Mental Health. During this period of centralization, mental health leaders and their allies simultaneously mobilized the consent and support of the American public to condemn the warehousing of the mentally ill. This chapter then outlines the processes and institutions by which the American political structure put the tools of science and technology to work in the field of mental health care. It depicts the legal, political, and economic arrangements through which new mental health technologies were developed, became available to the American public, and resulted in arrangements that will be characterized as supporting systems in the chapters on the passage of the Community Mental Health Centers Act.

Chapter 2 describes how the mental health elite designed a technocratically feasible alternative to warehousing: the comprehensive community mental health program. Through the instrument of President John F. Kennedy's Task Force on Mental Health, the mental health leaders provided the president with a legislative package acceptable to the general public.

Chapter 3 argues that despite the opposition of the AMA, Congress adopted a nonincremental approach to the nation's mental health. The act itself is described.

In Chapter 4 the process of drafting the regulations and standards for the Community Mental Health Centers Act illustrates the centralized nature of the mental health establishment.

Chapter 5 describes the impact of a presidential electoral mandate and of bureaucratic initiative on the passage of the staffing grants for the comprehensive community mental health centers.

Chapter 6, the epilogue, encapsulates the legislative modifications of the centers act and the current status of this national program.

In a summary analysis, chapter 7 maintains that the concept that explains the major policy shift from warehousing to community mental health care is the model of oligopolistic partisan mutual adjustment.

# Community Mental Health Legislation

# 1

# The Federal Politicization of Mental Health

In 1854, President Franklin Pierce vetoed the "12,225,000 Acre Bill," proposed by Dorothea Dix, which would have set aside public lands to assure humane treatment of the indigent and insane. Pierce replied that such action would usurp the action of the individual states. The states, responding to Miss Dix's documentation of the plight of the mentally ill, took responsibility for their care. Thus, the mentally ill became a state charge.

Over the next century, state mental institutions evolved into isolated facilities where long-term or even lifetime stays were the norm. The development of the asylums reinforced the stigma attached to mental illness and placed the care of the mentally ill outside the mainstream of general medicine and the local community. In addition to treating psychotic adults, state mental hospitals came to serve as repositories for persons for whom the community had limited resources: the aged, the alcoholic, emotionally disturbed children, and adolescents. Miss Dix's reform had become malignant.

From 1844 until the 1920s, most psychiatrists worked in state mental hospitals. By 1920 professors of psychiatry recognized the inadequate care given in the hospitals and encouraged residents to provide care in the community. New pyschiatrists then began to move into private practice with part-time service in the community and public facilities for the mentally ill. Philanthropic organizations, such as the Commonwealth Fund, encouraged young residents to provide care in mental clinics.

In the 1940s it was clear to psychiatric leaders in the armed forces and their congressional allies that there was a need to develop and to organize the capacity and willingness of all relevant decision-makers and institutions (not simply of some central agency) to cooperate in a broad societywide effort to identify, understand, and develop new technological skills in the research and care of the mentally ill.

By 1946 some members in the mental health leadership were committed to the concept of community care. However, they possessed neither the technology nor the control over the political process to enact a congressionally acceptable policy of community care. Methodically, they proceeded to develop that technology and the necessary political power.

In the late 1950s the professional mental health leadership recognized the need to communicate to the public that community care was tech-

1

nocratically supportable and to call for change. They created the Joint Commission on Mental Illness and Health to assess formally the mental health technology and to educate the public on the issue of the need for more adequate care of the mentally ill. Concomitantly, they involved the representatives of the widest possible range of interest groups in the United States. Their efforts were capped by successful mental health legislation in the 1960s under two presidents.

This book explores the development of a federal political base that supported the shift from custodial care in state mental hospitals to treatment in the community through federal programmatic and financial intervention. It examines over the years 1940 to 1963 the causal interlocking reasons for the development of political forces that resulted in the Community Mental Health Center Act of 1963: (1) the public climate of concern about the quality of mental health care, (2) the mental health leadership, (3) the maintenance of a national mental health establishment through the control of fiscal incentives, (4) the production of a resulting technocratic base of operations, buttressed by specific pressure groups, and finally, (5) the leadership's mobilization of political consent.

The federal politicization of mental health modified the constraints imposed by the political climate of the forties and fifties. The "political climate"—the public's collection of values, beliefs, and symbols—in the 1940s affected the decisions of government leaders and professionals concerned with changing the type of care for the mentally ill in three ways.

1. The stigma attached to mental illness prejudiced the American public and its elected representatives against its victims and their treatment. Solutions to mental illness were not discussed in the political forum. Mental illness was regarded as a problem of deviancy, not of medical illness. The American public avoided mental illness; it did not confront the need for its proper treatment. Americans had relegated their mentally ill to the backwaters of asylums—state mental hospitals.

2. The AMA and its supporters in the Congress resisted federal financial intervention into the training of medical personnel and the provision of services for all Americans as "socialized medicine."

3. The Congress wished to respect states' rights and state control over the delivery of mental health services.

The mental health leadership, in less than two decades, modified these beliefs and symbols about the mentally ill.

## The Origins of NIMH Leadership

The men and women who directed the development of a federal base of support for mental health were strongly committed to providing better care for the mentally ill. This moral imperative combined with technological knowledge to assure a centralized base of power from which to pursue deliberate and orderly solutions to this immense problem. Political theorist Chester Barnard has hypothesized that for such movements to succeed, leaders who are driven by "moral creativeness" and possessed of technological proficiency are required. "The strategic factor in cooperation generates leadership," he writes. That leadership "is the name for relatively high personal capacity for both technological attainments and moral complexity combined with propensity for consistency and conformance to moral factors of the individual." [1]

The leaders of the movement for active federal participation in mental health met these specifications. The major leader to emerge within the federal executive ranks was a psychiatrist committed to the moral purpose of ensuring humane care for the mentally ill and trained in the technology to carry out his purpose.

Dr. Robert H. Felix, who recalled recently that he and his colleagues "gave a damn for people," understood that he and his allies would have to garner incentives to bargain for implementation of mental health technologies.[2] Felix was to become the director of the National Institute of Mental Health and, from that position, develop a cadre of institutional leaders. Before that, he had joined with professional and lay groups to provide the political support and technological arguments for the congressional committees who could authorize federal support.

Robert Felix had grown up with William and Karl Menninger on the Kansas plains. He graduated from the University of Colorado in 1930. As a resident in Colorado under psychiatrist Dr. Frank Ebaugh he came to share his mentor's commitment to community care and revulsion against the condition of state mental hospitals. Felix would later call upon his Colorado colleagues to back his position before Congress when he became the director of the National Institute of Mental Health.

In 1933, Felix joined the Division of Mental Hygiene of the US Public Health Service, headed by Dr. Walter Treadway. The Division of Mental Hygiene represented the federal government's first step into mental health. It had been spawned by national concern for addicts and also carried out studies in addiction. The early concerns of the division were not with the devastating psychoses, but rather with addiction, crime, delinquency, the condition of mental hospitals, and the emotional consequences of immigrating to the United States. Within two years, Congress enlarged the scope of the division, renaming it the Division of Mental Hygiene and adding additional authority to study the prevalence, prevention, and treatment of nervous and mental diseases. The primary work of the division, however, remained addiction throughout the thirties and into the forties.

In 1935 the government built its first hospital for narcotic addicts near

Lexington, Kentucky, and followed with a second one three years later, near Forth Worth, Texas. With these resources and a small headquarters staff, the division undertook pioneering studies of drug abuse, while at the same time laying the groundwork for a larger national effort in mental health. Felix served at Lexington and moved up from the ranks. By 1942 he had completed his Master of Public Health degree at Johns Hopkins University with a thesis on the organization of a national mental health program. "More a dream than a thesis," he recently mused. The events of World War II, however, were to make Felix's dream a reality. Congressional concern over the psychiatric needs of American men, which surfaced during World War II, were to lead to a national program.

Aside from the high rate of psychiatric disorders resulting from the war itself, more men were rejected for the services due to psychiatric disorders than the total number fighting at the peak of the war in the Pacific. In addition, the demand for psychiatrists for the military services had so reduced their numbers in state mental hospitals that mental care was even more inadequate than before the war. In short, the war had called dramatic attention to the problem of mental disorders, pointing up the need for a national mental health program.

In 1945, Surgeon General Thomas Parran asked Felix to design such a program. Felix, now assistant chief of the Public Health Service's Hospital Division, met with the chief psychiatrists of two military services: Dr. William Menninger, army; Dr. Francis Braceland, navy; and Dr. Jack Ewalt, who was a consultant to the air force. Together, they would rework Felix's Hopkins thesis under his direction.

The four men were friends and also members of the newly formed Group for the Advancement of Psychiatry (GAP), the young radicals of the American Psychiatric Association who, wanting more than just the improvement of the state mental hospitals, promoted community care.[3] Sidney Saperstein drafted Felix's revised paper into a legislative bill, H.R. 2550.[4] In 1946, Representative Percy Priest (D-Tenn.), chairman of the Subcommittee on Health and Sciences of the Committee on Interstate and Foreign Commerce, introduced the National Mental Health Act, later known as the Priest bill. Lister Hill, the junior senator from Alabama, obtained the cosponsorship of distinguished senators from both parties for the Senate's bill, S. 1160. Senator Claude Pepper held the hearings in the Senate and took the bill through the Senate.

Witnesses were called from the leaders of the psychiatric profession, especially those committed to the treatment of mental disorders in the community, and those from other walks of life, who testified favorably for the bill. Occasioned by the catastrophic number of psychiatric casualities of World War II, supported by the massed weight of testimony orchestrated by Felix, Hill, and Priest, the bill was enacted into law, with only one dissenting vote in the House, and with unanimous approval of the Senate. The act was signed by President Truman on July 3, 1946.

The 1946 National Mental Health Act established the National Institute of Mental Health as the national focal point of concern, leadership, and effort for the mentally ill. The legislation of the Seventy-ninth Congress mandated the Public Health Service: (1) to foster and aid *research* relating to the cause, diagnosis, and treatment of neuropsychiatric disorders; (2) to provide for the *training* of personnel, for the award of fellowships to individuals, and for grants to public and nonprofessional institutions; and (3) to *aid states* in the prevention, diagnosis, and treatment of neuropsychiatric disorders through grants and technical assistance—by establishing clinics and treatment centers to carry out pilot and demonstration programs.

By providing training grants to institutions as well as training stipends and fellowships to individuals, the act went further than any previous health legislation. It was consistent with previous legislation in that it offered direct assistance to the states, a type of support used in two previous health programs: venereal disease control and tuberculosis control.

The act also provided for the creation of a National Advisory Mental Health Council, specifically charged with the responsibility of reviewing applications for research and training grants, and advising the surgeon general on all programs of public health services where mental health matters were concerned. The council had the supportive service of study groups organized by psychiatric-social scientific disciplines. The members of this council were not to be government officials, except for two ex officio members, one designated by the secretary of defense, and the other by the administrator of veterans affairs. The other members were psychiatrists and prominent citizens.[5]

Over the next decade the council assisted, checked, and in at least two instances, with the aid of Senator Hill and Representative John Fogarty of Rhode Island, directed Dr. Felix to adopt programs that he initially did not favor: the development of pharmacology and the psychiatric training program for the general practitioners. The council served as the public mechanism both to direct the development of mental health technology and to provide political links between the NIMH professionals, universities, professional organizations, philanthropic interests, and citizen groups.

After observing the council's operations for nearly a quarter century, Felix concluded in 1971 that it had produced a more significant effect on the direction and growth of the mental health program than any other provision of the 1946 legislation. "The quality of individuals selected to serve on this group, their dedication and sound advice from the very beginning, have involved the professional and nonprofessional public and have brought their concerns and needs into the institute's plans and operations." [6]

Historically, the council has served as a professional-citizen constituent base. Members of the major psychiatric interest groups have served on it: the American Psychological Association, American Psychiatric Association, National Committee Against Mental Illness, National Association for Mental Health, universities, and state mental health authorities.

The evolution of the professional-citizen constituent base for the NIMH occurred through the collaboration of Felix and the council. That evolution was abetted by the institute's directing mental health programs by means of fiscal patronage provided by the coalition of Washington health leaders.


**The Washington Health Syndicate**

Truman signed the National Mental Health Act the day before the Fourth of July holiday in 1946, and Congress adjourned the next day without funding the act. Not to be delayed, Felix obtained a grant of $15,000 from the Greentree Foundation to enable the council to meet and to initiate the program. In 1947 the Congress enacted the first appropriation. In April 1949, NIMH became fully operational when the Division of Mental Hygiene of the Public Health Service was abolished and NIMH became a part of the National Institutes of Health in the Department of Health, Education, and Welfare (HEW).

Felix was to become a top leader in the administration. He subscribed to the view that a good deal of the burden of legislative leadership for the executive branch in his special area depended upon himself and his staff. He was a participant in what Elizabeth Drew has termed "the Health Syndicate: Washington's Noble Conspirators." [7]

The decisions that affected the government's expanding role in medical research depended upon men and women in positions of great power in Washington: Dr. James Shannon, director of the National Institutes of Health; Senator Lister Hill, chairman of the Labor and Public Welfare Committee, which provided the money; Representative John Fogarty, chairman of the House Appropriations Subcommittee; Mrs. Mary Lasker and Mrs. Florence Mahoney, philanthropists who contributed to campaigns of politicians who favored medical research. The philanthropists supported Mike Gorman, a skilled lobbyist and the executive director of the National Committee Against Mental Illness, in developing data that compared the cost to the economy of various diseases to the cost of concerted research efforts to overcome them. In addition, Gorman provided valuable staff work to key congressional leaders. He became known for "doing his home-work."

Shannon combined his professional standards with his political instincts for the purpose of expanding "the obviously inadequate federal medical research base of the early 1950s." [8] In 1953 he joined forces with Fogarty and Hill to double the NIH budget.

From that year on, the three men drew up budgets deemed appropriate by the professional elite in the NIH. Felix also was part of that elite. Shannon included technical information in the reports justifying increased appropriations and marshalled medical scientists to support existing and new program positions.

Strategically, Fogarty and Hill proceeded in this fashion: Fogarty castigated the White House, the Bureau of the Budget, and HEW for sub-mitting a budget request for NIH lower than that which NIH had sug-gested. He elicited from the NIH officials, Felix among them, the amount they had initially requested, and corresponding to the one he had before him. He called for the "experts."

On his part, Gorman recruited as "citizen witnesses" such well-known physicians as Michael DeBakey and Karl Menninger. They offered "pro-fessional judgment budgets," in most instances higher than NIH's. The budgets were prepared by philanthropist Lasker and lobbyist Gorman, who lobbied all the members of the appropriation committees in both houses. Fogarty would then raise the NIH budget. His stature as an extremely knowledgeable appropriations chairman assured that he would be successful when the bill came before the full House.

Assisted by the same lobbying routine in the Senate, Senator Hill's tactic was to raise Fogarty's inflated budget still higher. Where new NIH programs could be funded under existing legislative authority, the tactics became specific. In "year one" the NIH directorship would raise the notion of the need for a specific program as "interesting," but not request money. Hill and Fogarty would ask for a technical report on the idea for "year two." In "year two" the NIH director submitted the report, and Fogarty and Hill appropriated the money for "year three." [9]

The Bureau of the Budget and HEW never publicly admitted that this strategy immobilized both their fiscal efforts in relation to NIH and checked the fiscal control of the president of the United States. It was important that Mrs. Mary Lasker and others were supportive to executive and legislative leaders alike, and this strengthened the hand of NIH in its negotiations. In the judgment of Dr. James Shannon "There was no conspiracy and that generally the secretary of HEW was as dissatisfied with the BOB proposal as was the director of NIH." [10]

From 1953 to 1960, "the health syndicate" expanded the federal financing of medical research nearly sevenfold, from $59 million to $400 million. Table 1-1 illustrates the fiscal growth of the National Institutes of Health from 1953 to 1960.

Participants in the health syndicate and the congressional hearings reveal that Fogarty and Hill did more than the secretary of health, education, and welfare during the Eisenhower administration to advance medical research.

**Table 1-1**

**Appropriations for the National Institutes of Health, Fiscal 1950-60**

| Fiscal Year | Estimate | House Allowance | Senate Allowance | Appropriation |
|---|---|---|---|---|
| | | (In thousands of dollars) | | |
| 1953 | 55,005 | 53,833 | 58,982 | 59,030 |
| 1954 | 56,340 | 61,586 | 72,153 | 71,153 |
| 1955 | 71,128 | 77,393 | 85,143 | 81,268 |
| 1956 | 90,314 | 89,773 | 113,416 | 98,458 |
| 1957 | 126,525 | 235,525 | 183,007 | 183,007 |
| 1958 | 190,183 | 190,183 | 226,783 | 211,183 |
| 1959 | 211,183 | 219,383 | 320,577 | 304,393 |
| 1960 | 294,279 | 344,279 | 480,604 | 404,000 |

Source: House Report No. 321, 87th Congress, 1st Session, 1961.

*The Effect of the Health Syndicate on NIMH*

The appropriations process of the health syndicate greatly influenced the development of NIMH as a pluralistic establishment. How pluralistic will become clearer when the incentives Felix used are enumerated. For the moment it should be noted that although Felix and NIMH benefited from the strategy of the health syndicate, Felix had to bargain with members of the syndicate. Key bargains struck with Mary Lasker and Mike Gorman were necessary to obtain increased appropriations.

Lasker pushed NIH directors to translate basic research into applied services. The fact that Felix designed and maintained a psychiatric organization that promoted applied research and demonstration services was consistent with her desires. Gorman was also sympathetic to Felix's revulsion toward traditional care in state mental hospitals. "My hidden agenda," he said recently, "was to break the back of the state mental hospital." [11]

Two major events in the programmatic development of NIMH demonstrate how Felix had to accommodate himself to the Lasker-Gorman pressure. The first event was their move to emphasize psychopharmacology. By the mid-1950s, European physicians were employing new tranquilizing drugs in treating mental illness, a breakthrough that had become known in this country, especially to Lasker and Gorman. They pressured Felix to direct NIMH funds to evaluate this new modality. Felix, however, was faced with NIMH scientists who were reluctant to begin the suggested massive study immediately because they felt it was premature. Felix himself may also have had reservations, because the institute had been increasing its work in psychopharmacology before 1957. Despite Felix's lack of support for a major psychopharmacology effort, Gorman gained Hill's and Fogarty's support. In the 1957 appropriations, Congress earmarked $2 million in additional funds for psychopharmacology. Gorman's witnesses in congressional hearings urged Congress to fund a multihospital, nationwide evaluation of the new drugs, to be undertaken by NIMH. With the earmarked funds, Felix established a Psychopharmacology Service Center. By 1960, when the effectiveness of the drugs had been demonstrated, Felix had become an ardent supporter, because they provided the technology needed to stabilize patients cared for in the community. In 1957, however, he accepted the bargain of additional funds for psychopharmacology research but not a redirection of NIMH's then current funds.

Felix also accepted the redirection of some training funds to non-psychiatric personnel. Gorman wanted more funds for training psychologists, nurses, and psychiatric social workers and for providing psychiatric training for general practitioners. In this instance, Felix may not have disagreed with Gorman and Lasker, but he faced contrary pressures from within the institute and from the American Psychiatric Association. Despite those pressures, the Gorman-Lasker axis convinced Congress to direct NIMH to fund training of all mental health personnel, not just psychiatrists.

Concealing their differences, Felix and the syndicate members presented a solid front to the members of Congress, other than Hill and Fogarty. By 1963, NIMH was the fourth-ranking institute in appropriations. Table 1-2 provides the fiscal comparison.

*The Technocratic Base and Constituents*

The organizational growth of NIMH was accompanied by other conflicts and compromises.[12] Felix, Shannon, Lasker, Gorman, Hill, and Fogarty modified their positions in order to gain each other's support. In this process, Felix and his allies in the mental health professional leadership and politicians established a technocratic base for a major national policy shift in the 1960s. This base was realized not only in the creation and the maintenance but the expansion of the National Institute of Mental Health under Felix's direction. The politics and technology revolving around the base led to the passage of the Community Mental Health Centers Act.

**Table 1-2**

**Fiscal 1963 Appropriations for NIH—By Institute**

| Institute | Inst. Profess. Judgment | Citizen Expert Judgment | Present Budget | House | Senate | Appropria- tion |
|---|---|---|---|---|---|---|
| | | | (In thousands of dollars) | | | |
| Gen. Res. and Services | 196,720 | | 147,826 | 155,826 | 161,826 | 159,826 |
| Cancer | 157,100 | 210,460 | 139,109 | 150,409 | 158,409 | 155,742 |
| Heart | 143,221 | 215,754 | 127,278 | 143,398 | 149,398 | 147,398 |
| Mental Health | 160,745 | 175,150 | 126,899 | 133,599 | 148,599 | 143,599 |
| Metabolic | 107,568 | 118,710 | 91,921 | 98,721 | 105,721 | 103,388 |
| Neurology | 91,913 | 125,000 | 71,206 | 77,506 | 86,506 | 83,506 |
| Allergy | 75,800 | | 59,342 | 62,142 | 68,142 | 66,142 |
| Dental | 20,308 | 24,294 | 17,199 | 19,199 | 22,199 | 21,199 |

Source: Compiled from Hearings and Reports House and Senate Labor-HEW Appropriations Subcommittees on Fiscal Year 1963 Appropriations.

## The NIMH Program

From 1948 to 1962 the NIMH under Felix's leadership accomplished three program objectives—the promotion of research, the development of manpower training, and the demonstration of new services—primarily through grants and contracts. Research, training, and services formed "NIMH's three-legged stool," a metaphor that came into use to point up that, unlike the rest of NIH, NIMH's responsibility was not confined to supporting research.

In 1962, 85 percent of the total NIMH appropriation supported grants for research, training, and community and technical assistance to nonfederal settings: universities, research and training institutions, and state and local mental health institutions and agencies. These organizations depended upon NIMH for partial financial support.

Through the grant use of the federal dollar, NIMH developed programs that drew a complex family of diverse disciplines into the mental health field—the biological, the clinical, the behavioral sciences. The resulting collaborative efforts both in research and in the application of research knowledge resulted in the emergence of an improved technology in the mental health field.

From its inception in 1948 until the end of fiscal 1962, the National Institute of Mental Health supported nearly three thousand research projects, a total of over $120 million in awards, in the substantive areas of mental retardation, child mental health and development, schizophrenia, depression, alcoholism, aging, drug addiction, and psychopharmacology.

During the same period the institute directed a major portion of its total effort to the problem of mental health manpower. The institute first supported the graduate training of the four core major professional groups: psychiatry, clinical psychology, psychiatric nursing, and psychiatric social work. Faced with the manpower needs in the field and with public pressure, as reflected in congressional mandates, the institute expanded its training program to general practitioners (promoted by Lasker and Gorman), occupational and recreational therapists, the clergy, psychiatric aides, and mental health attendants.

The institute supported 1500 training projects, whose awards totaled approximately $185 million. Eighty percent of the awards went to colleges and universities; approximately one-half of that sum went to medical schools. As of 1962, every major medical school's department of psychiatry, all the major graduate departments of psychology, graduate schools of social work, and graduate schools of nursing received some support through a training grant from the institute.

It is not surprising that, given such a financial impetus, the number of persons in the core mental health professions increased over 250 percent between the 1950s and 1960s, while the grand total in all health professions increased about 30 percent over that same period. The crucial political aspect of this financing is that the research and manpower programs provided NIMH with constituencies in the universities and the professions.

Felix recruited a staff of consultants to work with the representatives of public and private mental health organizations. Their function was to communicate research findings and to advise and assist in their application to treating mental illness. Collectively, these consultants served as a bridge between the research laboratories and the mental health practitioners —those who worked directly with mental patients and those engaged in the administration of clinics, mental hospitals, general hospitals, day centers, and other community facilities concerned with the care of the mentally ill. New knowledge from research that might be put into clinical practice or used to improve mental health services administration was critically analyzed. The most promising new information was translated into mental health treatment practices, with further evaluation in clinical settings through special studies and demonstrations.

To expand the existing community mental health services into a comprehensive system of mental health care, states were encouraged to adapt new treatment techniques. Some of the new or improved services were designed to meet the special needs of individual population groups, such as the aged, the alcoholic, and the juvenile delinquent.

Several special techniques were developed to disseminate new information in regard to the conduct of mental health services and to demonstrate the application of clinical techniques developed from research findings.

Demonstrations were implemented primarily in areas where the needs for new and improved treatment procedures had not been met. The demonstrations focused on the translation of new knowledge into treatment practices or the implementation of recently developed treatment practices in new settings.

Intensive workshops, called technical assistance projects, were started in 1955. They were designed to disseminate to state mental health representatives new information on the application of modern principles and of methods to administer mental health service programs. These technical assistance projects were planned with representatives of, and financed by, the National Institute of Mental Health. The projects were pilots of programmatic elements of the subsequent community mental health centers' inpatient care, outpatient care, partial hospitalization, emergency services, and consultation and education of caregivers in the community.

The Health Amendments Act of 1956 provided NIMH with new authorization (Title V) to develop improved methods for the care and treatment of mentally ill persons. NIMH, at the direction of Congress, used Title V authority to launch research and demonstration programs in such areas as aging, crime, delinquency, drugs and alcoholism, as well as clinical services provided in the community.

Another set of incentives available to the institute were the grants to states. The National Institute of Mental Health administered the mental health grant-in-aid to states from 1948. As constituted, this program was administered under authority of former Section 314(c) of the Public Health Service Act. Grants that states must match dollar-for-dollar were made to the agency in each state designated as the "mental health authority." Funds were made available to assist states in prevention and control of mental illness through establishing, maintaining, and expanding community mental health services.

In fiscal 1948, a minimum grant of $20,000 was made to each state, with the states expending a total of more than $1.6 million of grant-in-aid funds. The state community mental health programs expanded, and additional funds were appropriated to stimulate further activity on the part of the states in community mental health. The minimum grant to each state in fiscal 1955 was reduced slightly, but the total amount expended by states increased to $2.3 million. Further increase in grant appropriations enabled the minimum grant to be raised to $65,000 in fiscal 1962, and the total of grant funds expended by the states to $6.6 million.

The states utilized the grant funds primarily to develop and to assist in the operation of mental health services, including clinics. The federal funds were but "seed money." These programs provided a wide variety of mental health services to a full range of mental health patients, including the mentally retarded. As a consequence of the grants to states, as well as funds from vocational rehabilitation, many of the states were already in the business of providing community mental health services prior to the federal Community Mental Health Centers Act in 1963. The technology was in place.

From its inception in 1948 until the end of fiscal 1962, the NIMH supported four hundred projects through its mental health project grants program. The projects clustered around the areas of mental retardation, child health and development, juvenile delinquency, schizophrenia, depression, alcoholism, aging, drug addiction, and psychopharmacology.

NIMH was also tied into the Hill-Burton program, which could authorize the construction of special facilities for chronic disease, including mental illness. Although in the period 1947-62, the total federal expenditure under the Hill-Burton program was approximately $1.8 billion, only about 3 percent, or $59.6 million, had been used for construction of beds and facilities for care of the mentally ill. The Hill-Burton program had been authorized primarily to assist general hospital facilities, with only minimal support to mental health facilities. In large measure, most of the construction support provided had been confined to psychiatric wards in general hospitals.

## Mobilization of Consent

Felix and his psychiatric allies mobilized the states, the NIMH staff, and Congress for a national mental health program. Through grants and public relations, Felix helped to create in many states the separate mental health "authority" which had control over the appropriations for mental health care. Before that, in most states, the state health authority gave second priority to appropriations for mental health care. The formal organization through which the newly created mental health authorities related to Felix and to the surgeon general was the Council of State and Territorial Mental Health Authorities. The council convened annually to advise Felix and also to obtain his direction. It became another constituent pressure group—a significant one, because in many states the mental health budget was the single largest item. Like the other mental health pressure groups, the mental health authorities participated in the legislative process and exerted major influence on the NIMH administration.

Felix was more than entrepreneurial director of the National Institute of Mental Health, however. He had a person-to-person rapport with his staff. The philosophy he advocated—in the tradition of the Public Health Service Corps—was commitment to patient care in the community.[13] He selected staff who shared his commitment and encouraged them to feel that they were integral partners in the decision making of the institute.

Testimony given before congressional appropriations committees shows that the NIMH leaders helped to shape congressional and public attitudes to an acceptance of a national mental health program.

The process was additive, one of continuing education and improved communication. Testimony in the late 1940s and early 1950s reflected public indifference, emotionalism, or ignorance about the real nature of mental illness. Some members of Congress found untenable the idea of committing intelligent individuals to mental correctional institutions; others were appalled at the existing institutional conditions. The early dialogues between the professionals and Congress often resulted in misunderstanding. The specialized language of the mental health scientists bewildered the layman, whose questions, in turn, were often simplistic, revolving around explication of simple terms.

By the mid-1950s, communications had improved dramatically. Mental health, high in reader appeal, was a popular topic in newspapers and in a spate of magazines, scholarly and slick. The press was producing an increasingly knowledgeable public.

Voters could now understand that money must be spent to solve this critical problem. Congressmen, reacting to their constituencies, became quasi-experts. Witnesses before committees became extremely communicative, no longer confining themselves to layman's language. Complicated statistical tables and research designs were introduced as evidence. Sophisticated staffs alerted congressmen to responsible action. The impasses of education and communication cleared; the government-supported mental health movement advanced in successive stages in the direction originally envisioned by Felix and his allies. The result was to change public attitudes more than any other development in the history of the mentally ill.

A 1950 National Opinion Research Center Survey revealed a lack of public sophistication about mental illness.[14] The majority of the respondents indicated that they knew that mental illness could be treated but this entailed special facilities, institutions, and the services of psychiatrists. They were unaware of the range of illnesses and pessimistic about the possibility of recovery. They said that they would not act or feel normally toward a former mental patient even though they did not learn of his illness until they had known him for some time without noticing anything wrong about him.

A survey conducted in the late 1950s indicated that one in every four Americans had felt the need for help with emotional problems, and one in every seven had sought that help.[15] The problem of stigma against mental illness still existed, but mental health information had helped the public recognize and seek help for their psychological problems.

In 1960 two investigators working in Baltimore, Paul Lemkau and

Guido Crocetti, found a greater public sophistication about mental illness than was apparent in the 1950s and greater community acceptance of emergency and home care services for psychiatric patients.[16] By 1960 it appeared that the American public did not universally reject the mentally ill, nor was it thoroughly defeatist about the prospects of treating mental illness.

## The Special Role of the Joint Commission on Mental Illness and Health

From 1955 the major political instrument through which technological advances in mental health were communicated to the public was the congressionally sponsored Joint Commission on Mental Illness and Health. Why and how did the Joint Commission function?

In February 1954, Gorman assisted the Council of State Governments in a meeting of the National Governors Conference on mental illness in Detroit, the first conference in the history of the country addressed to the status of mental health care in the states. The governors were concerned that mental health grants to states had decreased from $3.6 million in 1950 to $2.3 million in 1955, and that the costs of care were rising.[17]

Dr. Kenneth Appel, president of the American Psychiatric Association, along with Gorman, Hill, Fogarty, and Priest, agreed on the need to assess the direction of the mental health movement. At the 1954 annual meeting of the American Psychiatric Association, Appel issued a call for a report, comparable to the Flexner study, on the status of mental health research and training. The Flexner Report was a 1910 study of medical institutions, made for the Carnegie Foundation for the Advancement of Teaching, that became a basic document in the reform and standardization of medical education and statutory requirements for physicians.

In February 1955, Senators Hill, John F. Kennedy, and other co-sponsors introduced S.J. Res. 46, which called for a mental health study act to provide for an objective nationwide analysis and reevaluation of the human and economic problems of mental illness. The Senate made it clear that the measure was not to be construed as interfering with or diminishing the more limited and specific programs and studies being conducted under the auspices of the National Institute of Mental Health; Felix's institutional base was not threatened. In March, Percy Priest held hearings on H.R. 3458 and H.J. Res. 230, the House counterparts to the Senate resolution.

Testimony before Priest's and Hill's committees indicates in kaleidoscopic fashion the agenda reflected in the final Joint Commission report. Felix highlighted the importance of NIMH in research, training, and community mental health programs.[18] Dr. Winfred Overholser, of St. Elizabeth's Hospital, spoke to the decreasing prospects for release of patients with advancing years of residence in a hospital. He suggested treatment of patients in the community as economical. "It is not only a question of emptying the hospital or reducing the load, not only restoring the patient to his family, but making him again a productive unit in society."[19]

Although Gorman emphasized the importance of the states' efforts, he voiced the concern of the governors that to maintain custody of patients, rather than to offer treatment, would lead to impossible budget situations. He noted that state expenditures for mental illness had increased more than 300 percent in ten years. Gorman also called attention to the cost of mental illness to the patient and his family as well as to public agencies.[20]

Dr. Daniel Blaine, medical director of the American Psychiatric Association, introduced to Congress the concept of the community mental health center. He explained that it was a new approach to organizing all mental health resources in a geographical area, including the mental hospital, general hospital, outpatient clinic, and public health prevention activities. The concept included active case finding, "working back in the homes to pick up cases and treat them there," Blaine said. He pointed out that such organizations had been tried in Canada and England, and that while mental health professionals were aware of the concept and experimentation with it, it apparently was unknown to laymen—including governors and legislators. Blaine suggested that the federal government fund experimental programs based on the concept.[21]

Dr. David B. Allmann, member of the Board of Trustees and chairman of the Committee on Legislation of the American Medical Association, testified that both the AMA and American Psychiatric Association in June 1955 concluded that a commission be formed with two basic objectives:

(a) to make a rational survey of all aspects of the present status of resources and methods of diagnosing, treating, and caring for the mentally ill and retarded, both within and outside of institutions; and (b) to formulate, on the basis of the survey, a feasible program for the fundamental improvement of our methods and facilities for the diagnosing, treatment, and care of the mentally ill and retarded.[22]

"What the Flexner Report did for medical education is what we hope to accomplish with the Joint Commission on Mental Illness and Health."[23] Allmann recalled that there had been great public interest in the movie *Snake Pit* and popular magazine exposés, and that demands for reform were growing.

Dr. Leo Bartemeir challenged the concept of the mental hospital as the primary tool for treating the mentally ill and pointed out that technology existed for new types of treatment: halfway houses, community care, new drugs, family reeducation.[24]

The American Nurses Association and the National Association for Mental Health supported H.J. Res. 230. Dr. Francis Braceland, then chief psychiatrist for the Institute of Living in Hartford, Connecticut, stated: "I think that with this new survey we begin now phase two." [25] (The establishment of NIMH was the first phase.) He wanted to convert mental hospitals from custodial to treatment institutions—to providing the care that would prepare patients to return to the community. Material on community mental health clinics from the publications of the NIMH was introduced into the record. Dr. Filmore H. Sanford, executive secretary of the American Psychological Association, obtained from Congressman Heselton the commitment that the bill specify that behavioral scientists would participate in the study—anthropologists, clinical and social psychologists, sociologists, political scientists, and economists.[26] Organized labor and the states testified on behalf of the bill.

After two months of consideration, all bills related to the act were reduced to H.J. Res. 256, passed by the House of April 21, 1955 and reported to the Senate by Hill on July 14, 1955. Without a dissenting vote, the Eighty-fourth Congress passed the Mental Health Study Act (P.L. 182) on July 28, 1955. The law required NIMH to establish a joint commission of Congress, which would report directly to Congress each year, to plan and conduct a thoroughgoing reevaluation of the nation's approach to mental illness.

Felix selected Jack Ewalt, then treasurer of the American Psychiatric Association, as the commission's director.[27] The selection, made with the APA's blessing, was based partly on Ewalt's previous experience with the First Hoover Commission. He had watched the commission's work filed away; little had happened. Consequently, from the inception of the Joint Commission, Ewalt built in ways of communicating and implementing its recommendations.[28] He expanded the number of interest groups from the AMA and the APA to a whole range of groups representing a cross section of society and government, from the American Academy of Neurology to the United States Department of Justice.[29] Ewalt intended to direct these pressure groups to influence favorable public opinion.

Each representative, nominated by his interest group but acting independently within the commission, would travel around the country once a year. He would speak to local and state constituents about the commission's work and obtain their feedback. Ewalt wisely decided to give special recognition to the American Legion. He obtained a grant from the Legion to publish the final report called "Action for Mental Health."

He did so in order to avoid the charge that the report was part of a "commie plot." In the hearing in which Ewalt gave the final report, one congressman raised such a charge. Ewalt pointed out that the American Legion had paid for the publication of the report currently before the congressman.[30] Thus, the charge was completely deflated. The accusation was never raised again about the work of the Joint Commission and its final product. The commission operated on the principle: to win public confidence, first confide in the public.

In his yearly progress report to Congress, Ewalt stressed the policy direction of the commission. He promised in the first report that the commission would provide "a comprehensive view of the many facets of the problem, and permit the Joint Commission to recommend to Congress, the states, and the mental health professions a course of action best calculated to achieve maximum progress in the future."[31] He went further in the second report, expressing the hope that the commission's recommendations would result in the development of a "rationally planned, cooperative, nationwide mental health program."[32] He saw it as a commission duty to stimulate action at national, state, and community levels.

Thus, in its scientific aspects, the Commission is concerned with theory, its testing, and its validation. In the area of moral or social responsibility, however, it is concerned with practice—what works for the improvement of mental health, what produces better results in treating mental illness, where we have failed, and what should be done next.[33]

In the second report, Ewalt also broached the concept of the neighborhood health center, available to people on the basis of their residence and manned around the clock to give emergency psychiatric services when needed.

The commission funded studies on patterns of patient care, nonpsychiatric community resources for mental health, the role of schools in mental health, the role of religion in mental health, along with others, including some on economic issues. They were published in a monograph series.

Several members of the commission served on NIMH's National Advisory Mental Health Council and shared ideas with NIMH staff. Through the five years of the commission's existence this communication created a common perception about what was needed.[34]

While the commission did its work, Felix was propagandizing; he tried to give the general public the impression that the commission's recommendations would result in the development of a nationally planned, coordinated nationwide mental health program. In his third report to Congress, Ewalt refers to Amsterdam's Querido, whose work centered on the care of mentally ill patients in the community.[35]

When it finished its work in 1960, the Joint Commission recommended:
(1) that federal, state, and local governments' spending for public mental
health services in state mental hospitals should be doubled in five years
and tripled in ten; (2) government loans, scholarships, and especially
income tax relief should be granted immediately to encourage the pursuit
of higher education by young people, particularly in the health professions;
and (3) the present system of state mental hospitals should be abandoned
and replaced by a totally new concept of mental health care, based upon
community centers for patient treatment, psychiatric units in general
hospital for short-term, inpatient treatment, open communities for those
acutely mentally ill but who could be rehabilitated, and chronic disease
centers for long-term illnesses of all kinds.[36] The first and third points were
inconsistent, because Ewalt had to accommodate interest groups within
the commission which were either pro state mental hospitals or pro community mental health.

*Action for Mental Health,* the final report of the Joint Commission,
proposed an expansion, combined with certain shifts of emphasis, in the
research grant program, "ably administered at present by the National
Institute of Mental Health." Second, the commission advocated a further
evolution in the delivery of mental care. It recommended to the American
public that mental hospitals be reformed as mental health centers; that is,
as part of an integrated community service, the centers were to include
outpatient and aftercare facilities, as well as inpatient services.

In the area of federal-state relations, the commission suggested two
important principles: "the Federal Government, on the one side, and
state and local governments, on the other, *should share in the cost* of
services to the mentally ill"; and "the total Federal share would be arrived
at, in the series of graduated steps over a period of years, the share being
determined each year on the basis of state funds spent in a previous
year." [37]

Ewalt recognized the inadequate funding base for state mental health
programs and desired total federal financing for the cost of services for
the mentally ill. He and his colleagues stressed the immediate need for
national action to focus medicine, professional services, education, and
research on the needs of patients.

Before the report was issued, Felix already had set the stage for the
development of a national mental health program focusing on community
mental health facilities. On November 23, 1960, he requested an increase
of $244,000 for the NIMH community services programs in order to fund
demonstrations of comprehensive community mental health facilities.

The testimony of Felix, in his role as director, and Ewalt, as head of
the Joint Commission, documents (1) the salutary use of drugs in treating
the mentally ill, resulting in a significant reduction of patients in mental

hospitals since 1955; (2) dramatic improvement in the area of recruitment and training of hospital manpower; (3) improvement in mental health facilities and in the care of patients; and (4) public acceptance and reliance on geographical centers for mental care.

The mental health elite and their lobbies had made a persuasive case for the care of the mentally ill to become a national responsibility. As a combined force these groups knew how to attract the attention of people who could influence the crucial decisions—the elected decision-makers. These politicians, adhering to the values that had developed in the 1950s concerning the care of the mentally ill, believed that they should enact a program that would constitute a radical shift in the delivery of mental health care in the United States.

This exploration of the relevant institutional and organizational considerations affecting the development of a new mental health technology occurred at a time when there was a shift in values from those of an individually oriented society to those of a society in which the public interest was becoming a matter of more than rhetorical concern. The technological base developed in the 1950s as a result of an understanding of how the existing state mental hospital system functioned and how it had failed in the past.

The proponents of a mental health technology sought financial support from public revenues while, at the same time, their own assessments informed the political system. Their contributions were supplemented by those of organized groups that saw the prospects of their own causes benefiting by such technological change. They recognized their stake in the developing technology around care of the mentally ill in the community and were prepared to make their way through the legislative and appropriations processes of the federal government. They valued the technological development in terms of its likely impact upon a fairly narrow set of objectives and interests. At the same time, they had to present their position within the social and legal environment that structured the eventual policy output in the 1960s.

Certainly, the central question asked of this technology was what it would do to the economic or institutional interest of those who were deciding whether or how to exploit it. Although the emerging technology appeared to represent a merely incremental advance, it was, in fact, an obviously radical departure from precedent. That technology converged with various technologies and with related social, political, and cultural trends that were present in the 1950s.

Close collaboration with the mental health leadership made it possible for the American political system to participate in the technological shift in the mental health care system of the 1960s. That system had been prepared for this by the efforts put forth in the 1950s. This specific mental health technological development—both in its direction and velocity of change—was largely determined by incentives offered by a mental health leadership, centered in the National Institute of Mental Health, attuned to the general political and intellectual climate of the late 1950s. Through the Joint Commission's work from 1955 to 1960, the notion of community-located treatment was communicated to the general public and attracted widespread public interest efforts to increase the public's understanding of mental health problems. This preceded and accompanied the shift that occurred in the delivery of mental health care during the early 1960s. Increased public participation also evolved.

The decisions regarding mental health technology in the 1950s were often political in character. They became, therefore, the responsibility of the politically responsible branches of government and of those politically accountable bodies specifically entrusted with legislative responsibilities in this narrowly circumscribed area.

The scientific priorities established in the National Institute of Mental Health were determined by social and political priorities as well as by purely scientific considerations. This was particularly applicable to applied science technology and to policy-oriented programs. The technological assessment that occurred in the National Institute of Mental Health was continually subjected to independent criticism and to countervailing pressures from several knowledgeable congressmen. Consequently, it became less of a weapon for individuals and groups defending their own narrow self-interest, although this did occur to some extent.

As the National Academy of Sciences has stated:

Much can . . . be said for having Congress intimately involved throughout [technology assessments] since it is the views of congressmen and of their affected constituents that will ultimately determine the fate of many important policy recommendations emerging from assessment activities.[38]

The political history of the NIMH appears to indicate that the technology assessment, sponsored by Congress, could result in legislation that would provide a system of care for the mentally ill in the community. This phenomenon would emerge because a combination or a balance had been achieved between the technological capacity to provide for a new service system in the country and a political understanding and willingness in the decision-making structure to implement such a new care system. How this decision-making structure operated is the subject of the following chapters.

By 1960 the mental health leaders in the NIMH were in the position to promote a major service program. They had politically powerful sponsors in Congress and multiple constituencies, all of whom believed that NIMH was underfunded. These mental health leaders, especially Felix and Gorman, had bought a consensus through their provision of economic incentives through NIMH programs. It was unlikely that the mental health constituencies dependent upon NIMH would oppose a program advocated by Felix. Opposition would have to occur from outside the constituencies.

### Interest Groups Represented on the Joint Commission on Mental Illness and Health

American Academy of Neurology
Academy of Pediatrics
American Association for the Advancement of Science
American Association on Mental Deficiency
American Association of Psychiatric Clinics for Children
American College of Chest Physicians
American Hospital Association
American Legion
American Medical Association
American Nurses Association and the National League for Nursing (Coordinating Council of)
American Occupational Therapy Association
American Orthopsychiatric Association
American Personnel and Guidance Association
American Psychiatric Association
American Psychoanalytic Association
American Psychological Association
American Public Health Association
American Public Welfare Association
Association for Physical and Mental Rehabilitation
Association of State and Territorial Health Officers
Association of American Medical Colleges
Catholic Hospital Association
Central Inspection Board
Children's Bureau
Department of Health, Education, and Welfare
Council of State Governments
Department of Defense, U.S.A.
National Association for Mental Health
National Association of Social Workers
National Committee Against Mental Illness

National Education Association
National Institute of Mental Health
National Medical Association
National Rehabilitation Association
Office of Vocational Rehabilitation
United States Department of Justice
Veterans Administration

# Notes

1. Chester I. Barnard, *The Functions of the Executive* (Cambridge, Mass.: Harvard University Press, 1968), p. 288.

2. Interview with Robert H. Felix, 17-18 February 1972.

3. Interviews with Francis Braceland (14 April 1972), Jack Ewalt (12 April 1972) and Robert H. Felix (17-18 February 1972).

4. Robert H. Felix to Bertram S. Brown, 12 October 1971.

5. The National Mental Health Act, 79th Congress, 1946.

6. Robert H. Felix, "The Challenges—Past, Present, and Future," Address at Twenty-Fifth Anniversary of the National Mental Health Act, Washington Hilton Hotel, Washington, D.C., 28 June 1971.

7. Elizabeth Brenner Drew, "The Health Syndicate: Washington's Noble Conspirators," *The Atlantic,* December 1967, pp. 75-82.

8. Interview with Dr. James Shannon, 22 March 1972.

9. Ibid.

10. From Dr. James Shannon, to Henry A. Foley, 31 March 1974.

11. Interview with Mike Gorman, 24 March 1972.

12. The information for this analysis on the research, training, and service grants is a synopsis of "A Summary of PHS Mental Health Programs—Current and Proposed Legislative Authorities, April 5, 1963," NIMH Files in Appendix A. The tabulation of the appropriations for NIMH programs, excluding Hill-Burton funds, are in Appendix I. The appropriations indicate the fiscal growth of NIMH.

13. Interview with Dr. Stanley Yolles, 23 March 1972.

14. *Confidential Forecast of the Results of the Survey of Popular Thinking in the Field of Mental Health.* National Opinion Research Center, University of Chicago, Survey No. 272, September 1952.

15. Gerald Gurin, Joseph Veroff, and Sheila Field, *Americans View Their Mental Health* (New York: Basic Books, Inc., 1960).

16. Paul V. Lemkau, and Guido M. Crocetti, "An Urban Population's Opinion and Knowledge About Mental Illness," *American Journal of Psychiatry* 118, no. 8 (February 1962): 692-700. For a review of all surveys on public opinions and attitudes, see Harold P. Halpert, *Public Opinions and Attitudes About Mental Health,* Research Utilizations Series No. 1045, 1963, U.S. DHEW Public Health Service National Institutes of Health.

17. Interview with Mike Gorman.

18. *Hearings Before A Subcommittee of the Committee on Interstate and Foreign Commerce, 84th Congress.* First Session on H.R. 3458 and H.J. Res. 230, 8, 9, 10 and 11 March 1955, p. 7.

19. Ibid., p. 16.

20. Ibid., p. 35 and *Hearings* of Senate Subcommittee on Health, p. 76.
21. *House Hearings,* pp. 76-77.
22. Ibid., pp. 104-105.
23. *Senate Hearings,* p. 29.
24. Ibid., p. 34.
25. *House Hearings,* p. 124.
26. Ibid., p. 146.
27. Interview with Dr. Walter Barton, medical director of the American Psychiatric Association, 16 March 1972.
28. Interview with Dr. Jack Ewalt, 12 April 1972.
29. Joint Commission on Mental Illness and Health, *Action for Mental Health* (New York: Basic Books, Inc., 1961), pp. 306-307.
30. Interview with Ewalt.
31. Dr. Jack Ewalt, "Digest of First Annual Report Joint Commission on Mental Illness and Health Year 1956" (Cambridge, Mass.: Joint Commission on Mental Illness and Health), p. 8.
32. Dr. Jack Ewalt, "Second Annual Report of the Joint Commission on Mental Illness and Health," p. 4.
33. Ibid.
34. Interview with Mrs. Ruth Knee, 19 February 1973.
35. Dr. Jack Ewalt, "Third Annual Report of the Joint Commission on Mental Illness and Health," p. 14.
36. *Action for Mental Health,* pp. vii-xxiv.
37. Ibid., p. xxi.
38. National Academy of Sciences, *Technology: Processes of Assessment and Care* (Committee on Science and Astronautics, U.S. House of Representatives, July, 1969), p. 108.

## Bibliography

*Books*

Barnard, Chester I. *The Functions of the Executive.* Cambridge, Mass.: Harvard University Press, 1968.
Deutsch, Albert. *The Mentally Ill in America.* New York: Doubleday, Doran and Company, Inc., 1938.
Fein, Rashi. *The Economics of Mental Illness.* New York: Basic Books, Inc., 1958.
Frohlicks, Norman, Joe A. Oppreheimer, and Oran R. Young. *Political Leadership and Collective Goods.* Princeton, N.J.: Princeton University Press, 1971.

Goffman, Erving. *Asylums*. Garden City, N.Y.: Doubleday Anchor Books, Inc., 1961.

Gurin, G., J. Veroff, and Sheila Field. *Americans View Their Mental Health*. New York: Basic Books, Inc., 1961.

Olson, Mancur, Jr. *The Logic of Collective Action*. New York: Schocken Books, 1965.

Price, Don K. *The Scientific Estate*. Cambridge, Mass.: The Belknap Press of Harvard University Press, 1965.


*Articles and Addresses*

Clark, Peter B. and James T. Wilson. "Incentive Systems: A Theory of Organizations," *Administrative Science Quarterly* 6, no. 2 (September 1961).

Drew, Elizabeth Brenner. "The Health Syndicate: Washington's Noble Conspirators." *The Atlantic,* December 1967.

Felix, Robert H. "The Challenges—Past, Present and Future." Address at Twenty-Fifth Anniversary of the National Mental Health Act, Washington Hilton Hotel, Washington, D.C., 28 June 1971.

Strickland, Stephen P. "Integration of Medical Research and Health Policies." *Science,* 17 September 1971.


*Reports*

Albee, George. *Mental Health Manpower Trends*. Joint Commission on Mental Illness and Health, Monograph Series, no. 3. New York: Basic Books, Inc., 1959.

*Technology: Processes of Assessment and Care*. A Report of the National Academy of Sciences, Committee on Science and Astronautics, U.S. House of Representatives, July 1969.

The Joint Commission of Mental Illness and Health. *Action for Mental Health*. New York: Basic Books, 1961.


*Public Documents*

U.S. Congress. Committee on Interstate and Foreign Commerce House of Representatives, *Hearings on the Causes, Control, and Remedies of the Principal Diseases of Mankind,* 83rd Congress, 1st Session, part 4, 7, 8 and 9 October 1953.

U.S. Congress. *Hearings Before A Subcommittee of the Committee on*

*Interstate and Foreign Commerce, H.R. 3458 and H.J. Res. 230, 84th Congress, First Session,* 8, 9, 10 and 11 March 1955.

U.S. Congress. *The National Mental Health Act,* 79th Congress, 1946.

U.S. Congress. Senate Committee in Labor and Public Welfare, and House Committee on Interstate and Foreign Commerce, Public Law 182, *Mental Health Study Act of 1955,* H.J. Res. 230, 84th Congress, 1st Session, 1955.

U.S. Congress. Public Law 31, *Mental Health Amendments of 1967,* 90th Congress, 1st Session 1967.

U.S. Senate. Committee on Labor and Public Welfare, *Report on the Mental Health Study Act of 1955,* Report No. 870, 84th Congress, 1st Session, 1955.

*Seminar Papers*

Strickland, Stephen R. *Medical Research in a Political Setting.* Seminar Paper, Department of Political Science, The Johns Hopkins University, 31 May 1966.

*Interviews*

Dr. Walter Earl Barton, 16 March 1972.

Dr. Francis Braceland, 14 April 1972.

Dr. Jack Richard Ewalt, 12 April 1972.

Dr. Robert Hanna Felix, 17-18 February 1972.

Mr. (Mike) Thomas Francis Gorman, 24 March 1972.

Mrs. Ruth I. Knee, 19 February 1973.

Mrs. Florence Mahoney, March 1972.

Mr. Sidney Saperstein, June 1972 and September 1973.

Dr. James H. Shannon, 22 March 1972.

Dr. Stanley Yolles, 23 March 1972.

# 2

## The Politics of Presidential Initiative

The report of the Joint Commission on Mental Illness and Health clearly called for an expanded federal role in providing services for the mentally ill. It gave two conflicting plans for the expansion, however; it both recommended beefing up the state mental hospitals through federal subsidies, and it favored transferring support for services from the hospitals to community centers that could provide treatment for the mentally ill close to home. This chapter will detail how the president of the United States and the coalition of mental health leaders in Washington responded to and resolved the commission's confusing recommendations. Although slow to move on the recommendations initially, the National Institute of Mental Health became the pivotal agency in establishing a national program of care for the mentally ill. It was guided by a presidential inter-agency task force of policy advisors in developing legislation and mobilizing critical constituencies for political action.

### The Hiatus

The Joint Commission had focused national attention on a broad spectrum of issues related to mental health and illness, and by the time it had completed its report these issues were still fresh in the public mind. The time was ripe for political action. Top-level discussions about the commission's recommendations in the Department of Health, Education, and Welfare resulted in the dismissal of one of the commission's suggestions. HEW officials thought that a large-scale federal program directly supporting hospital care of mental patients would violate what they considered to be the intent of Congress—not to fund care of state hospital patients.[1] They also considered the proposal too expensive. For that reason, they decided that a federal-state initiative should focus on the support of a comprehensive mental health program that would emphasize the development of a continuum of services in states—including services for the prevention of mental illness, and for improved care, treatment, and rehabilitation of mentally ill persons. The NIMH was charged further with the responsibility for developing an approach that would, to the extent possible, utilize existing legislation and models of federal-state relations.

Initially, NIMH urged new legislation to implement aspects of comprehensive community mental health care and to increase funding for those aspects covered under existing legislation in the current and ensuing fiscal years.

During 1960 and 1961 a few staff members of the National Institute of Mental Health responded to the Joint Commission's report with a series of internal documents directed to the director of NIMH, the surgeon general, and the director of NIH. The basic response was that the proper goal for any federal, state, or local mental health program should be the improvement of the mental health of the people in the country through a continuum of services; it should not just center on the rehabilitative aspects of mental health programs, which had been a primary thrust of the recommendations of the joint commission.

An institute task force, chaired by Dr. Joseph Henry Douglass, responded to each of the commission's recommendations. It rejected the recommendation to triple the amount of funds for state mental hospitals; rather, the NIMH endorsed the principle of significant levels of federal financing of a total mental health program. The staff proposed an increase in the grant-in-aid program (former Section 314[c] of the Public Health Act), to support a total mental health program, including inpatient and outpatient mental health services.[2] The staff's responses may be characterized as incremental: NIMH made no effective or politically significant response to the report in terms of an innovative program. There was a hiatus from 1960 to the summer of 1961, the period between the action recommendations of the Joint Commission and the presidential initiative.

Unlike the NIMH staff, the National Advisory Mental Health Council did not take a position on the commission's proposal that the federal government and the states share in the cost of services to the mentally ill.[3] Federal activities in 1960 were centered in research, training of manpower, support of demonstrations, improvement of public health services, and construction of facilities. The issue of the federal role in direct patient services was a major policy innovation which demanded a substantial justification. This was particularly essential in view of the contemporary controversy surrounding the federal role in medical services to the aged.

Shannon, in his power position as director of NIH (to whom the NIMH was responsible), recognized that the establishment of a national program involving partial federal financing of care of the mentally ill was a social policy question with very broad ramifications. Such a policy, therefore, had to be determined at the political level, not by health professionals. Consequently, he declared that any program recommended as feasible by the NIMH staff would have to be consistent with public policy.[4]

Central decision making at the presidential level was the necessary element for a nonincremental innovative program.

**Presidential Decision Making**

In July 1960, the impact of the Joint Commission's report, mediated through the efforts of Mike Gorman, was manifested in a plank of the Democratic party;

> Mental patients fill more than half the hospital beds in the country today. We will provide greatly increased Federal support for psychiatric research and training, and community mental health programs to help bring back thousands of our hospitalized mentally ill to full and useful lives in the community.[5]

John F. Kennedy was faced with the task of formulating a policy responsive to the plank. To the mental health leadership, President Kennedy was "the right person at the right time. The essential ingredient in the creation of a national mental health program was the interest of the president." [6]

Once elected, however, Kennedy's task was complicated by the fact that members of his family—especially Eunice Shriver—wanted federal investment in the care of the mentally retarded, separate and distinct from a mental health program.

**The Mental Retardation Effort**

For political reasons, the mental retardation program and community mental health program were to emerge as separate titles in the final congressional bill.

The National Association for Retarded Children had formed in the 1950s. Triggered by parents despondent at the lacunae of mental health care facilities, it organized on local and state levels and eventually coalesced into a national group. Through the efforts of congressmen sympathetic to the association (especially Fogarty), the Congress authorized a limited expenditure of funds on a national level for retardation. John F. Kennedy was cognizant of this early program.

Upon the request of his sister Eunice Shriver, President Kennedy made the study of mental retardation one of his earliest priorities on taking office in 1961. Some months later he appointed a panel of distinguished researchers to implement his commitment to placing the problem in a proper national perspective, defining it, and resolving it through viable federal action. Twenty-seven leaders in health, education, welfare, social sciences, law, and other fields were called upon to analyze the problem and to present to the president their recommendations. Eunice Shriver also served on the panel. Known as the President's Panel on Mental Retardation, its prime objective at that time was to be *A Proposed Program for National Action to Combat Mental Retardation*. The panel, whose director was Dr. Rick Heber, intensively researched the problem for over a year. It used four methods of study and inquiry that, while not identical, were similar to those of the Joint Commission.

1. All members were assigned to task forces on specific subjects, with advisors designated to work closely with them.

2. Public hearings were held in seven major cities. Public officials concerned with mental retardation, parents, teachers, representatives of related professions, and others reported on local and state programs, spelled out weaknesses, and made recommendations.

3. Panel members and their advisors visited England, Sweden, Denmark, and the Soviet Union to study and benefit from methods of care and education of the retarded abroad.

4. The members reviewed, in large part, the literature and recent studies on retardation and collated their findings.

The panel's two-hundred-page report included ninety-two recommendations. Its clear conclusion was that mental retardation was a national, social, and economic problem affecting some 5.4 million children and adults, involving from 15 to 20 million family members in the United States.

In brief, the panel's report, when submitted to President Kennedy, proposed a series of measures to control a critical health issue, brought sharply into national focus:

1. enhancement of public awareness and encouragement of greater interest and participation in a nationwide effort to combat mental retardation by all levels of government, by communities, by foundations, and by private organizations;

2. fostering of additional basic and applied research in causes and prevention;

3. provisions of larger numbers of teachers, researchers, and other specialists needed for study and services;

4. support of preventive health measures, especially in the "high-risk" low-income groups that produce a disproportionately large number of the mentally retarded;

5. extension and improvement of special education for the retarded;

6. increase in vocational rehabilitation services;

7. protection of the civil rights of mentally retarded persons; and

8. securing of better coordination among federal programs and between them and nonfederal activities.

The panel proposed to the president a comprehensive program that included augmentation of activities under present authority, legislative modification of existing law, and new legislative authority to promote additional activities.[7]

Throughout the panel's study and subsequent recommendations to President Kennedy, many members involved (especially Eunice Shriver) argued against the participation of the psychiatric discipline in the program under design. They felt strongly that, in the past, mentally retarded persons had received second-rate service from the psychiatric profession. Consequently, they did not want psychiatrists to be involved in a national program concerning the mentally retarded; specifically, they did not want NIMH to administer any retardation program. Aware that the influence of some of the members of the panel implied budgetary cutbacks to the NIMH, Felix helped to maneuver such programs into other parts of HEW, especially the National Institute of Child Health and Human Development.[8]

A key staff person detailed to the task force on mental retardation from the National Institute of Mental Health was Dr. Bertram S. Brown.[9] Brown provided staff work on the panel and, at the same time, served as the NIMH liaison to the White House. At the request of Meyer Feldman, special assistant to the president, in the fall of 1962, Brown and Michael March of the Bureau of the Budget consolidated the recommendations of the panel on retardation and the efforts of the president's task force on mental health.[10] Intensive budgetary and legislative review of both efforts ensued, resulting in the president's separate mental retardation and mental health legislative packages.

## The President's Interagency Task Force
## on Mental Health

John F. Kennedy asked his staff in the White House for an assessment on the mental retardation effort related to the Joint Commission, which was evidence that the lobbying activities of the mental health interest groups had been successful. This was because Lasker and Gorman had access to the president.[11] Kennedy had read *Action for Mental Health*.[12]

Kennedy and Feldman knew that effective power had to be extracted out of other men's self-interest, especially in the Washington bureaucracy.[13] Consequently, they designed a task force that involved the national mental health leadership, as well as the Bureau of the Budget. Whether the mental health issue was primary or secondary, Kennedy sought the means (a task force) and men in government to assure that these men used their personal pattern with its stress on open options and on close control.

On the advice of Feldman, Kennedy set up an Interagency Task Force on Mental Health to respond to the Joint Commission's report with a bold new program. He appointed HEW Secretary Celebrezze as chairman and included the secretary of labor and the administrator of the veterans affairs. He requested the Bureau of the Budget and the Council of Economic Advisors to assist in the work. Kennedy asked the task force members to answer five questions in order to plan appropriate federal action:

1. What should be the federal role in mental health and what responsibility should remain with the states, localities, and private groups?

2. If broadened federal activity is warranted, through what channels should it be directed?

3. What emphasis should be given to federal activity in mental health in relation to support for more general health programs?

4. What rate of expansion in public programs for mental health services and research is consistent with the present and prospective supply of trained manpower?

5. In the mental health field, should relatively greater encouragement be given to strengthening institutional services or noninstitutional programs, including means for bringing the cost of noninstitutional services within the financial means of a larger number of people? [14]

Secretary Celebrezze delegated the chairmanship to Boisfeuillet Jones, special assistant to the secretary for health and medical affairs in HEW.[15] Jones included the NIMH leadership in the task force and asked the NIMH to develop specific proposals for implementation, of its particular mission and recommendations for possible activities by other governmental units. Jones viewed 1964 as the best year in which to take federal action in response to the joint commission's report.

Felix told his staff on April 23, 1962, that assisting the President's Interagency Task Force was the most important task the institute faced.[16]

### The Bureau of the Budget's Role

A critical contribution to the interagency task force was made by the Bureau of the Budget's Robert Atwell, the BOB's budget examiner for NIH. The bureau (reorganized into the Office of Management and Budget in the Nixon administration) coordinates the monetary requests of various federal agencies and, after modifications by the president, presents to Congress a budget detailing proposed expenditures and sources of income. The bureau also was authorized to "revise, reduce, or increase" requests. Staff of the bureau then, as now, advised the president on matters of administrative organization, supervised financial programs, controlled rates of congressionally authorized expenditures, reviewed agency programs and proposals before Congress for compatibility with presidential policy, and prepared veto messages for financial bills unacceptable to the president. The BOB staff was both powerful in relation to agencies' budgets and knowledge of the agencies' programs. Atwell was no exception. He had read the Joint Commission's complete studies. In his judgment, those studies totally discredited the system of state mental hospitals; yet the commission's report emphasized improved institutional services. There was little attention to noninstitutional services and virtually no discussion of how to make it possible for a much larger proportion of the population to afford the cost of noninstitutional care. While Atwell agreed that the improvement of institutional services was extremely important, he argued that it was even more crucial to stress the noninstitutional services in the future.[17]

## The NIMH Task Force

During the previous spring, Atwell had asked Dr. Stanley Yolles, NIMH deputy director, what the institute was doing about the Joint Commission's recommendations. At that time, the NIMH staff was doing very little about the report.[18] Atwell stirred NIMH to respond to the commission with position papers. Felix set up an NIMH task force under Yolles to develop a comprehensive program in response to the Joint Commission's report. The members of this task force were almost all officers in the Public Health Service, including Drs. Bertram Brown and Allan Miller, and were imbued with a public health philosophy. They emphasized mental health care to patients in the community, care as part of the total health care system, and care available to the general population in specific geographical zones. Pressured by the presidential demand, this task force was now to serve as the technological supporting staff to the President's Interagency Task Force on Mental Health and Illness.

Yolles's task force did the staff work for the interagency task force. The motivating force of that staff was a public health commitment. This staff had the personal experience and approach of the Prince George's demonstration program in Prince George's County, Maryland. Set up in 1949 to deliver a range of community services, it was considered a successful experimental model. Through its regional offices, NIMH had tried to interest local communities in the concept during the 1950s. The exported experiment, when applied to community health clinics, proved unsuccessful, because the clinics failed to develop fiscal and administrative linkages with the total health system in local communities.

The two most important factors in the development of a proposal by the NIMH task force were its members' public health training and access to the findings of the Community Services Branch of NIMH. (There were more staff members holding Masters of Public Health degrees in the NIMH in 1959 than in any other division of the Public Health Service.) Not only did the members of the NIMH task force possess a public health philosophy, they had also been traumatized by their work experience in state mental hospitals.[19] By 1960 the bits and pieces of the concept of community mental health care were coming together. The institute had used the Prince George's community-oriented program as a training ground for Yolles, Brown, and Miller and had conducted demonstrations of community mental health care. The staff and members of the task force considered three major issues:

1. Should the mental health centers developing in the states be promoted as the major mechanism or system in the delivery of mental health services?

2. To what extent should NIMH stress ambulatory care versus institutional care?

3. What should be the relative responsibilities of the voluntary sector, the state, and the federal government?[20] Yolles developed the position that the mental health center was to be the major ambulatory delivery system funded by the federal government. The financing would be in the form of permanent subsidiaries, not in the form of "seed" money. A federally financially-assisted system of approximately two thousand centers would provide NIMH with the same type of political power that the postal system possessed. A center located in every congressman's district would increase the patronage power of Congress and enhance the political viability of NIMH as the coordinating agency of this new system.[21]

The National Advisory Mental Health Council collaborated with Yolles in the design of the community mental health center proposal. The council members—especially Gorman, Ewalt, and Dr. George Tarjan, who served the Kennedy family in the White House—considered that the community mental health center program would become an essential component of the National Institute of Mental Health.


**Members of the President's Task Force**

Boisfeuillet Jones was the chairman of the presidential task force. He had created and organized the medical center at Emory College, where he was the vice-president and administrator of health. In Eisenhower's second term, he had served on the National Advisory Health Council. In the spring of 1960, he was chairman of the Consultants on Medical Research, which issued the "Jones Report" for the Senate Appropriations Committee. He became special assistant to the HEW secretary, first under Ribicoff and later under Celebrezze.

The other members were Felix of NIMH, assisted by his deputy, Yolles. Daniel P. Moynihan represented the Secretary of Labor; Manley, Veterans Administration; Atwell, the Bureau of the Budget; and Rashi Fein, the Council of Economic Advisors. The membership of this task force may be divided into two types: the political appointees (Jones, Moynihan, and Fein) on the one hand, and the professional bureaucrats (Felix, Yolles, Manley, and Atwell) on the other. Jones had direct access to the White House and, in fact, as special assistant to the secretary (Health and Medical Affairs), ran the HEW health programs.

In his government work in New York under Governor Averell Harriman, Moynihan had witnessed the decline in admissions to state mental hospitals due to chemotherapy and the need for treatment programs in the community.[22]

Fein had written one of the Joint Commission's monographs, *The Economics of Mental Illness*. He had argued that the proportion of the gross national product that could be directed to the support of mental health services depended upon the will of the citizenry. Society could not refuse to spend on mental illness and health.[23]

Felix consistently represented the professional concerns of the psychiatric professions. Yolles would continue to support planning for a comprehensive mental health program, begun in his own task force in the NIMH. Manley, the representative of the Veterans Administration, was supportive. Atwell was committed to a national federal effort, but one that would not fund state mental hospitals, as recommended in the Joint Commission's report.

The NIMH career professionals, Felix and Yolles, were concerned primarily with the problems of the human estate: What was professionally appropriate in the care of the mentally ill? Financial and political concerns were secondary. Felix recalls that he thought that the clinical, budgetary, and political issues should be left to the professionals in each field. In politics, they were Jones and Moynihan; on budgetary matters, Atwell; and on financing, Fein.[24] Felix was realistic enough to know that he had to listen to those who could judge what the nation would support.

Jones, Moynihan, and Fein, the political appointees, were, in Moynihan's opinion, responsible for informing the career professionals of what the administration could accept. The political appointees were running the task force but depended upon Felix and the other career professionals to tell them what was professionally appropriate as a national mental health program. However, the political appointees did check the NIMH views with independent experts. The experts agreed that the proposed program was desirable and, in terms of medical knowledge, feasible. They did not consider the NIMH as "visionary." [25]

All the decision-makers in the task force were against incarcerating the mentally ill and wanted the mentally ill treated in the mainstream of medicine and in the local community.

The task force was characterized by supportive relationships; its members became a cohesive group, and each was provided an environment of trust, which removed his inhibitions and encouraged him to behave creatively.

## The Deliberations of the Task Force

On April 13, 1962, the president's task force discussed the comprehensive mental health program proposed by Felix and Yolles.

The National Institute of Mental Health, said Felix and Yolles, had concluded that the mentally ill could be better served through community mental health centers and not through large state mental institutions isolated from community life. There would always be a hard core of patients who would need institutional care, but it was felt that populations of these institutions at that time (about 525,000) could be greatly reduced in the next generation.

The substitute for the state mental hospital was to be the comprehensive community mental health center, offering both inpatient and outpatient services, including a general diagnostic and evaluation service, an acute inpatient service, outpatient services, day-care services, night-care services, emergency services, rehabilitation services, foster-home supervision, consultation, public information, and education services.

All of these services were to be provided under the roof of a single center, or they might be attached to the psychiatric ward of a general hospital, or be geographically dispersed throughout the community. These decisions would be at the option of the local community, consistent with a state plan, subject only to the requirement that there be, from the point of view of the recipient of the services, a single integrated program requiring only one point of entry—the one-stop service station.

These centers and their affiliated programs typically would be staffed by over one hundred professional psychiatrists, psychologists, social workers, nurses, therapists, counselors, and supporting clerical services. In addition, private psychiatrists, psychologists, and other professionals would offer part-time services to the center on a fee basis, in exchange for which they might be required to perform certain emergency functions for the center without compensation, in much the same way that the physicians in a community staff the emergency units of general hospitals on a rotating basis. The proportion of staff and private practitioners would vary according to the desires of the community and the management of the center.[26]

In the ensuing discussion, Manley of the VA expressed the idea that the report was very good, the best thing so far; "hope it all comes about." [27] Atwell felt that the concept was a refreshing one, a good departure from the final Joint Commission report, and hoped for a funding pattern different than the state-oriented Hill-Burton formula. Fein was concerned as to how to maintain state financing. He also viewed the center concept as more beneficial for the patient and the nation's economy. Felix advocated federal and state matching of financing based on the Hill-Burton formula. The political appointees and Felix agreed that the states had to be involved. Hill-Burton financing was the appropriate mechanism. Felix suggested the utilization of regulations and standards to control the type of program desired. Atwell expressed the need for standards of some sort to evaluate the new mental health program. Moynihan was interested in the challenge of eliminating mental hospitals and in developing new types of mental health manpower. There would never be enough psychiatrists. Blue-collar workers could not afford them. Felix agreed to Moynihan's points. Atwell was interested in the coordination of the Mental Retardation Panel and their effort. He felt that the manpower question remained the critical problem. Jones expressed the view that the program envisioned totally new community mental health legislation.

Jones, Moynihan, and Fein accepted the idea that NIMH knew what program was needed, and, in their own minds, "The CMHC program was reasonable." [28]

The public administration issue was whether to bypass the states completely or to give them assistance. In the president's task force, Jones, Felix, and Moynihan argued that it was politically and professionally inappropriate to bypass the states: politically inappropriate because such an action was counter to the pattern of the then current federal-state relations; professionally inappropriate because adequate care would have to be provided in many state mental hospitals until the goal of two thousand community mental health centers was reached (one per 100,000 population). Atwell argued that the states should be bypassed because they were an obstruction. Fein argued that the states were not in the position adequately to support the care of mental patients. Consequently, Fein had no objection to the position that financing mental health care should become a permanent federal subsidy.

The strategy of the mental health leadership and their allies was to "demonopolize" the state role in the provision of mental health services and attempt to establish a triad of federal, state, and local support for mental health services. At this time, federal bureaucrats planned to blanket the whole country with comprehensive community mental health services.

Their intention was not to federalize the total program through its financing, but to obtain a degree of control through the resulting federal regulations and standards.

The task force agreed to the strategy and proposed the comprehensive community mental health center approach as the cornerstone of the president's program. Its specific recommendation was a categorical program in which there would be federal grants-in-aid to assist in the *construction* of comprehensive community mental health centers, including psychiatric units in general hospitals, with the goal of establishing five hundred such centers by 1970, and decreasing matching federal dollars to cover the initial operating funds for the centers.

The task force reasoned that without operating grants, states and local governments would not build the centers, because: (1) they couldn't afford to run them; or (2) if they built them, they would not provide comprehensive services; or (3) in the operation of a comprehensive program, they would screen out "charity patients" into the state hospital; or (4) they would run the comprehensive program but only by robbing other sectors (for instance, education).

To initiate a modern, effective mental health program for the nation, the task force also recommended:

1. additional grants to states for the planning of comprehensive community mental health programs; through the tactic of the "professional judgment budget," Felix had already obtained 1962 NIMH appropriations for such grants, known as the comprehensive mental health planning grants;
2. federal support to raise the level of patient care in state mental hospitals through grants to states for (a) demonstrations of new and improved techniques of patient care, (b) the replacement of obsolescent facilities (the hospital improvement program), and (c) inservice training for the staff of these institutions (hospital staff development program);
3. federal stimulation of and reinsurance for voluntary insurance programs covering the costs of mental illness;
4. federal support for the training of the additional professional and sub-professional manpower necessary for the large-scale attack on mental illness proposed in the report; and
5. continued increase in federal support of research in mental health.

The task force proposed these points in order to eliminate, within the next generation, the state mental hospital as it then existed.[29]

Clearly, the president's interagency committee had not been bound by the report of the Joint Commission. The members had departed from the commission report in a major respect: in the proposal that there be an intensive effort to eliminate, within a generation, the state mental institution, as it then existed, in favor of comprehensive community-centered mental health programs. This departure represented the best professional judgment of the National Institute of Mental Health and was tailored to the judgment of the political professionals on the questions of federal-state-local relationships and fiscal constraints. The proposals, taken together, represented something of a professional and political compromise between a massive effort to upgrade the quality of care in the mental hospitals and doing nothing for the hospitals by putting all the federal resources into the community mental health centers. Atwell reported to the director of the Bureau of the Budget that the construction of community mental health centers would be phased over the next eighteen years as follows:

> 1965-66— 50 centers
> 1967 — 75 centers
> 1968 —100 centers
> 1969 —125 centers
> 1970 —150 centers
> 1971-80—150 centers each year.[30]

## The President Resolves the Conflict

The work of the task force had raised several issues that, while neither mitigating the need for the program nor seriously disputing its feasibility, would require the intervention of the president. Did the proposal for community mental health centers adequately consider the issues involved in operating such centers? Secretary Celebrezze thought not. Was the proposed program feasible in terms of the supply of manpower? March of the BOB was adamant that the program was not feasible.

The issue of operating cost and the supply of manpower were considered within the Task Force and the BOB on the basis of rational-economic calculation.

*Operating Costs*

HEW and the interagency task force contemplated a diversity of sources to finance operating costs: state, local, and private, including a federal subsidy covering up to 50 percent of staffing costs (37 percent of operating costs) for each center on a declining basis for two or three years.[31] Consequently, the federal government would pay 20 percent of the estimated

$530 million operating cost for centers in 1970 and 30 percent of the total cost of $725 million for building and operating them.

The arguments in support of this position were: HEW had stopped far short of the recommendations of the Joint Commission that the federal government bear two-thirds of the costs of all mental health community clinics (and seven-eights of the increase for mental care over 1960 level). Instead, it proposed that the federal government bear 60 percent of the cost of building the mental health centers and also share in the *initial staffing* costs of a center. The partial HEW subsidy for staffing costs was designed to help communities get comprehensive centers started, but to stop short of a permanent subsidy.

The arguments against the position were: HEW visualized a major federal commitment to support the *construction* and, temporarily, the operation of community mental health facilities. The grants for staffing purposes, however, would contrast with the existing situation whereby HEW subsidized mental health care only through limited demonstration and research projects. It would also be inconsistent with the existing pattern in general hospitals (including mental hospitals) whereby Hill-Burton construction grants, but no federal operating subsidies, were provided.

Yet, even though a permanent subsidy might be eschewed, it was questionable whether communities would undertake to operate centers if there was no federal subsidy after the second or third year. Could the pattern of the fifteen- or twenty-fold increase in community mental health services between 1948 and 1961—with only $5 million of federal grants per year—be repeated on a large scale?

HEW and the interagency task force proposed the obligation of $330 million between 1965 and 1969 to build five hundred mental health centers in addition to $150 million for mental retardation facility construction. By 1970 the construction rate would be 150 mental health centers per year ($117 million) *plus* perhaps $50 million of mental retardation facilities. Would manpower be available to achieve the goal of five hundred mental health centers by 1970 (and possible two thousand by 1980)?

*Manpower Needs*

To man the facilities, HEW proposed that federal training outlays be increased nearly three and a half times, from $55 million in 1963 to $190 million in 1970, representing an increase from 46 percent to 66 percent in the proportion of federal funds to total training outlays. This would include Department of Labor outlays under the manpower development and training program to increase the employment of ancillary personnel from 100,000 to 180,000 by 1970.

The arguments for this position were: HEW estimated that, at a minimum, necessary employment in the four core specialities would be as shown in table 2-1.

HEW had considered the feasibility of making available this manpower. On the crucial question of shortage of psychiatrists, it was pointed out that the ratio of psychiatrists per 100,000 population had increased from 3.2 in 1949 to 7.1 in 1960; both HEW and the task force believed that even without a special effort, the upward trend would continue. The increase in the number of psychiatrists was being accelerated by NIMH through the

**Table 2-1**

**HEW's Estimates of CMHCs' Need for Mental Health Personnel**

| Specialty | 1950 | 1960 | 1970 | 1980 |
|-----------|------|------|------|------|
| | | (In thousands) | | |
| Psychiatrists | 5.5 | 13.0 | 23.5 | 36.0 |
| Clinical psychologists | 3.5 | 9.0 | 20.6 | 40.0 |
| Psychiatric social workers | 3.0 | 7.2 | 16.5 | 35.0 |
| Psychiatric nurses | 10.0 | 15.0 | 25.9 | 52.0 |
| Total | 22.0 | 44.2 | 86.5 | 163.0 |

retraining of 475 general practitioners a year. NIMH proposed to increase this number from 750 to 1500 per year.

The arguments against this position were: Attaining the HEW estimates would be exceedingly difficult. The number of psychiatrists would have to increase 80 percent by 1970, although the number of active physicians in the country would increase less than 20 percent. If all specialties continued to increase at the current rates, there would be more specialists than general practitioners by 1980; the trends toward specialization would then have to level off.

The number of social workers for psychiatric service in competition with public assistance, child welfare, and juvenile delinquency programs would have to rise 2.3 times between 1960 and 1970 to more than double their own employment. The capacity of the schools of social work was, however, not adequate to meet these needs. The employment of psychiatric nurses would have to rise 73 percent, about three times the likely increase in the total supply of professional nurses by 1970.

The shortage of psychiatrists was particularly crucial, because the ratio of active physicians per 1000 population could be increased very little by 1980, even with the proposed doctor training bill. If the proportion of psychiatrists was to be doubled at the same time that medical research was expanding rapidly, this would mean a reduction in the ratio of general practitioners and other specialists available to provide service to people with no mental illnesses. BOB projected the number of physicians per 100,000 population as shown in table 2-2.

The critical issue that could determine whether there would be a new national program, rather than a continuation of demonstration efforts, was manpower. The BOB's March maintained that there would not be enough psychiatric manpower for sustained national effort. Other members of the Bureau of the Budget, especially Atwell, disagreed, but their arguments

**Table 2-2**

**BOB Projections of Number of Available Physicians per 100,000 Population**

| Type of Physician | 1949 | 1960 | 1970 | 1980 with training bill |
|---|---|---|---|---|
| All active physicians | 128.4 | 125.9 | 125.4 | 127.3 |
| Psychiatrists | 3.2 | 7.1 | 11.2 | 13.7 |
| All other physicians: | | | | |
| Total | 125.2 | 118.8 | 114.2 | 113.6 |
| Research adm. | 2.5 | 4.0 | 8.9 | 12.1 |
| Clinical practice | 122.7 | 114.8 | 105.3 | 101.5 |

were not cogent enough to defeat March's position. March argued that more training funds of health professions should not be shifted to psychiatry. The issue remained unresolved in the Bureau of the Budget. In a White House meeting with March and his BOB superior, Hirst Sutton, Feldman decided in favor of raising the funds for the training of psychiatric professionals.[32]

The president resolved the issue of operating costs. Although Celebrezze felt that the states should initially pay to operate their programs, the president told him directly in November 1962 to put provisions for operating costs into the proposed legislation.[33]

Consequently, the design of the president's legislative package may be viewed as the outcome of hierarchical decision making in which the bargaining centered on the politically and professionally acceptable in the context of a common goal: care of the mentally retarded and mentally ill patient outside the state mental hospital.

**Political Mobilization**

The key question was, of course, the extension of the federal government's role, in conjunction with the states and localities, in the care of the mentally ill in the United States. While the staff of the institute fully recognized that the decision to develop a national community mental health program was a matter for the executive branch (of which they were, of course, a part) and the Congress, the NIMH leadership brought in professional and political allies to assure the success of their proposals.

Felix, Blaine, and Gorman also served as consultants to the policy committee of the Governors' Conference on Mental Health, November 9-10, 1961, in Chicago. The governors' policy statement, originally drafted in NIMH, called for federal, state, and local financing of community mental health services.

Jones, who attended on behalf of President Kennedy, assured the governors that Kennedy and his administration were carefully considering the Joint Commission's recommendation that the federal government pay part of the cost of care for the mentally ill. He told the governors that their deliberations would be extremely useful in helping the administration determine the ultimate role of the federal government.

Fogarty then gave the congressional mental health perspective.[34] His speech also reflected several themes that the allied mental health leadership would emphasize prior to the introduction of the CMHC legislation:

1. In drafting mental health legislation, from 1946 to 1960, the Congress had carefully restricted the role of the federal government to a stimulative one, by emphasizing research, training, and matching clinic grants to aid the states in developing additional ammunition for an all-out fight on mental illness.

2. Testimony before congressional committees, especially Fogarty's, indicated that the significant reduction in the mental hospital population load resulted from a number of factors: the introduction of new drugs, increased numbers of psychiatrically trained personnel in state hospitals, and the increased availability of new psychiatric facilities designed to serve patients in the community.

3. The care of the mentally ill continued to place a heavy load upon the states. Fifty states were spending approximately $1.2 billion annually for the maintenance and treatment of patients in state institutions for the mentally ill and mentally retarded.

4. The Joint Commission reported that only 20 percent of the mentally ill were housed in hospitals that provided active treatment rather than mere custodial care. Americans were spending too little on the treatment of the mentally ill in state mental hospitals; for four or five dollars a day there would be no therapeutic miracles.

5. Fogarty states: "Most of all, the Joint Commission Report stated over and over again that to improve the care of the mentally ill, all levels of Government—Federal, state and local—must join together in a united effort."

6.

In the years ahead, I want to see this problem of mental deficiency licked, and I don't care who . . . does it—the Federal Government, the state government, private research foundations. However, I have a strong suspicion that it is going to take all of these to do the job. . . . The problem of mental illness cannot be limited to any one jurisdiction of Government. The mentally ill person who breaks down in Rhode Island, Nebraska or California, or here in Illinois, is not only a citizen of that particular state—he is a citizen of this entire country, and his loss is a loss to all of us. In these crucial times, our country can hardly afford the staggering losses of manpower exacted by mental illness.[35]

The National Institute of Mental Health had prepared a position paper endorsing the major findings of the Joint Commission's report and had outlined a federal-state matching program for over the next five years.

The conference asserted that a modern approach required great public investment in research, training, prevention, and treatment, and that this added investment should be borne not only by the states, but increasingly by local governments—where the problem must be met—and by the federal government—which must regard the conservation of productive life as fostering its greatest natural resource.

On March 23, 1962, Fogarty increased the political pressure. He reviewed the progress of the NIMH and excoriated the executive branch for not presenting an integrated program consistent with the final report of the Joint Commission.[36]

Between January 10 and 12, 1962, in their annual conference with the surgeon general, the State and Territorial Mental Health Authorities had agreed to (1) federal aid in mental illness and health, (2) Hill-Burton funds for community mental health facilities, (3) community planning for coordinating services for the mentally ill, and (4) allocation of new appropriations for care of the mentally ill.

In the fall of 1962, Jones met with the AMA's Council on Mental Health. The members questioned the task force's staffing grant proposal as government intrusion into the reimbursement pattern of physicians. As a political strategy to pick up support of the AMA, Jones coined the term "desocialization" of mental health care. To the charge of *socialized* medicine, Jones answered that the choice of public or private operation of the centers was for the local community to make. The community mental health center, in a very real sense, was an entirely "desocialized" alternative to, and substitute for, the state mental hospitals. There would be less of a socialistic flavor to the community mental health centers in the sense that they would be community rather than state operated. In addition, a large number of the centers would be privately operated (albeit publically subsidized).

Jones emphasized that the new national program would not just involve mental hospitals, but also the private sector, although local communities would overtax themselves in financing the initial years' costs of centers operation. Consequently, the federal government's initial financing of these costs, including physicians' salaries, was reasonable.[37] The council accepted his position and voted unanimously to support the staffing grant provisions in any proposed legislation. Throughout 1962 and 1963, Jones would continue to rally mental health groups in support of the community mental health and mental retardation legislation.

**Evaluation of the Task Force**

The 1962 President's Interagency Task Force on Mental Health significantly affected the development and content of the community mental health centers legislation. Before the presentation of the legislative package, members of the task force legitimatized ideas consensually agreed to in task force deliberations and mobilized support for the president's program. When the Congress debated the legislation, two members, Jones and Felix, were to form a formidable political-professional team allied with the mental health leadership.

In essence, the success of the Joint Commission depended upon the allied mental health leadership. The centers legislation derived from imaginative leadership at two levels: the NIMH professional leadership led in the technocratic development of improved care of the mentally ill; and the administrative leadership of the Kennedy appointees designed a fiscally and politically viable program developed in the interagency task force. The stage was set for the president to urge congressional action on a comprehensive community health program in which the federal government paid for the services costs, but not completely. Would Congress react favorably to this innovative approach?

# Notes

1. Report of NIMH Task Force on Implementation of Recommendations of the Report of the Joint Commission on Mental Illness and Health, 5 January 1962.

2. NIMH Position Paper on Report of the Joint Commission on Mental Illness and Health, August 1961.

3. "Suggested Modifications by NAMH Council to NIMH Position Paper on Joint Commission on Mental Illness and Health" to Special Assistant to Secretary, Health and Medical Affairs, DHEW, 20 September 1961.

4. Memorandum on Implementation of the Final Report of the Joint Commission on Mental Illness and Health from Director, NIH, James A. Shannon, M.D., 10 October 1961.

5. Plank adopted in the Platform of the Democratic Party, Los Angeles, July 1960, quoted by Senate President John E. Powers, Massachusetts, at Governors' Conference on Mental Health, Chicago, Illinois, 10 November 1961.

6. Interview with Dr. Stanley Yolles, 23 March 1972.

7. Bertram S. Brown, M.D., "The President's Mental Health Program," speech presented at Annual Meeting, Mental Health Association of Essex County, East Orange, New Jersey, 20 June 1963. Based on information and HEW Memorandum "Proposed Program for Expanded Mental Retardation Activities," 8 November 1962.

8. Interview with Felix, 18 February 1972.

9. Ibid.

10. Interview with Bertram S. Brown, M.D., 13 March 1972.

11. Interview with Boisfeuillet Jones, 3 April 1972.

12. Interviews with Ewalt, 12 April 1972; Barton, 16 March 1972; Braceland, 14 April 1972; Yolles, 23 March 1972; and Gorman, 24 March 1972.

13. Richard E. Neustadt, *Presidential Power* (New York: John Wiley & Sons, Inc., 1960), pp. 163-64.

14. Celebrezze, Wirtz, Gleason, Letter of Transmittal to the President from the Office of the Secretary, DHEW, 4 November 1962, p. 1.

15. Interviews with Van Stadden, 13 March 1972 and 7 April 1972.

16. Memorandum from R. H. Felix, M.D., to Chief, Community Services Branch; Chief, Research Grants and Fellowship Branch; Chief, Training Branch, NIMH, 23 April 1962.

17. Interview with Robert Atwell in January 1972, confirmed by Dr. Stanley Yolles, 23 March 1972.

18. Interview with Yolles, 23 March 1972.

19. Ibid.

20. Interview with Ruth Knee, 19 February 1973.

21. Interview with Yolles, 23 March 1972.

22. Interview with Patrick Moynihan, 12 June 1972.

23. "The annual direct and indirect costs of mental illness therefore can be estimated at the very minimum to be upwards of $2.4 billion." Rashi Fein, *Economics of Mental Illness* (New York: Basic Books, Inc., 1958), p. xii. In 1961, Atwell updated Fein's figures to $3 billion in "Staff Analysis of Report of the Joint Commission on Mental Illness and Health," 6 June 1961, p. 4.

24. Felix.

25. Moynihan. Ibid.

26. Abstracted from the "Yolles' Green Book," titled *A Proposal for a Comprehensive Mental Health Program to Implement the Findings of the Joint Commission on Mental Illness and Health,* April 1962.

27. Minutes of the Task Force, April-May 1962.

28. Interviews with Professor Rashi Fein, January-April 1972.

29. Celebrezze.

30. Robert Atwell, "Draft Memorandum to the Director of BOB re Proposals for the President's Mental Health Program," 1 November 1962.

31. All the figures for the following calculations were drawn from the "BOB Analysis of Proposed National Action Program for Mental Health," 3 December 1962. BOB obtained these figures from the Biometry Division of NIMH under Dr. Mort Kramer and the Division of Manpower Training under Dr. Eli Rubenstein.

32. Interview with Mr. Meyer Feldman, 19 August 1972.

38. Fein, and Jones.

34. John F. Fogarty, "Progress Toward Mental Health—A Joint Responsibility." Address to National Governors' Conference on Mental Health, 10 November 1961.

35. Ibid., p. 4-7.

36. House Report, 23 March 1962, of the Committee on Labor, Health, Education, Welfare Appropriations.

37. Jones.

## Bibliography

*Books*

Neustadt, Richard E. *Presidential Power*. New York: John Wiley and Sons, Inc., 1960.

Seidman, Harold. *Politics, Position and Power.* New York: Oxford University Press, 1970.

Sorensen, Theodore C. *Kennedy.* New York: Bantam Books, Inc., 1965.

Zisk, Betty H., ed. *American Political Interest Groups: Reading In Theory and Research.* Belmont, Calif.: Wadsworth Publishing Company, Inc., 1969.


*Memoranda and Reports*


Celebrezze, Wirtz, Gleason. "Letter of Transmittal to the President from the Office of the Secretary, DHEW," 4 November 1962.

Memorandum from Rashi Fein to Walter W. Heller, 21 November 1962.

Memorandum from R. H. Felix, M.D., to Chief, Community Services Branch; Chief, Research Grants and Fellowship Branch; Chief, Training Branch, NIMH, 23 April 1962.

Memorandum on Implementation of the Final Report of the Joint Commission on Mental Illness and Health from Director, NIH, James A. Shannon, M.D., 10 October 1961.

NIMH Position Paper on Report of the Joint Commission on Mental Illness and Health, August 1961.

Report of NIMH Task Force on Implementation of Recommendations of the Report of the Joint Commission on Mental Illness and Health, 5 January 1962.

"Suggested Modifications by NAMH Council to NIMH Position Paper on Joint Commission on Mental Illness and Health" to Special Assistant to Secretary, Health and Medical Affairs, DHEW, 20 September 1961.

The "Yolles' Green Book," titled *A Proposal for a Comprehensive Mental Health Program to Implement the Findings of the Joint Commission on Mental Illness and Health,* April 1962.


*Addresses*


Brown, Bertram S. "The President's Mental Health Program." Speech presented at Annual Meeting, Mental Health Association of Essex County, East Orange, New Jersey, 20 June 1963. Based on information and HEW Memorandum "Proposed Program for Expanded Mental Retardation Activities," 8 November 1962.

Fogarty, John F. "Progress Toward Mental Health—A Joint Responsibility." Address to National Governors' Conference on Mental Health, 10 November 1961.

Plank Adopted in the Platform of the Democratic Party, Los Angeles, July

1960, quoted by Senate President John E. Powers, Massachusetts, at Governors' Conference on Mental Health, Chicago, 10 November 1961.

## Public Documents

House Report, 23 March 1962, of the Committee on Labor, Health, Education, Welfare Appropriations.
U.S. House of Representatives. House Government Operations Subcommittee. Report No. 321, 87th Congress, 1st Session, 1961.

## Interviews

In addition to all the interviews of chapter 1,
Mr. Robert Atwell, January 1972.
Dr. Bertram S. Brown, 13 March 1972.
Professor Rashi Fein, January-April 1972.
Mr. Meyer Feldman, 19 August 1972.
Mr. Boisfeuillet Jones, 28 February 1973.
Professor Daniel Patrick Moynihan, 12 June 1972.
Mr. George Van Stadden, 13 March and 7 April 1972.

# 3

## The Politics of the Legislative Compromise

The Community Mental Health Center Act of 1963, a milestone in the history of the care of the mentally ill, was not to become law without a fight. Now that the President's Interagency Task Force had developed a proposal for a community centers program, mental health leaders shifted their attention to the legislative process. Powerful men in Washington pooled their effort and influence to devise a plan to convince Congress to take this historic step. Their task involved complex political issues whose solution called for bargaining ability and expertise in a variety of subjects.

Gorman, the spokesman for the philanthropists, was to be the coordinator for the legislative effort when it reached Capitol Hill. "The mosaic was coming together," he said recently in recalling the time. "It was becoming clear that we had to have an authorization for a community mental health program. *Action for Mental Health* had condemned the whole custodial mental health hospital system as malignant." [1]

Gorman had worked directly with Hill and Fogarty, who agreed that the Joint Commission's report demanded legislative attention. NIMH leaders Felix and Yolles and their allies in the White House—Brown, George Tarjan, Stafford Warren, Reginald Lourie, Jones, and Feldman—chose Gorman as the coordinator because he was the most skilled mental health lobbyist available. [2] The personal relationships of the psychiatric elite and their allies cemented the coalition.

In several meetings during April and May 1962 in the West Room of the White House, Gorman pressured Feldman and the president to propose legislation to satisfy Senator Hill, who wanted action in response to the Joint Commission's report after the one-year hiatus. In 1962, Hill and Fogarty had already appropriated funds to NIMH for allocation to the states, which were to use them to design comprehensive state mental health plans with emphasis on care in the community. Consequently, by 1963, when the president would call for legislative action, the mental health leadership was ready to go. The states were already planning.

Gorman was told to temporize. "We had to hold off on the mental health legislation because Jack Kennedy and Eunice Shriver, through Mike Feldman, said that there would be no presidential initiative until the Panel on Mental Retardation reported in 1962." [3] Also, the National Advisory Mental Health Council had not agreed on the design of the community mental health centers legislation to be proposed. Nor had the NIMH leadership tested the professional or political winds to determine the acceptability of the center concept.[4]

Hill and Felix were setting the stage for the centers legislation and "testing the winds." In testimony before Senator Hill, Felix pointed out that the technology existed to implement the Joint Commission's recommendations. "If the communities will enter into cooperation with the Federal Government and private foundations and agencies with the right good will, public mental hospitals as we know them today can disappear in 25 years," he said.

We are moving toward a new concept of community mental health in which the total comprehensive program is encompassed in centers strategically located in the community where . . . all the various types of emotionally disturbed patients can be handled in the community and can be referred back into the community at the earliest possible date.[5]

Hill responded: "More and more community mental health centers are beginning to be developed, as a result of this joint endeavor of the states and communities."[6] He listed thirteen states (Oregon, South Carolina, Utah, Wyoming, New York, Indiana, Connecticut, New Jersey, Minnesota, Virginia, Maine, South Dakota, and Wisconsin). These states and California had state mental health acts. He mentioned for the record that the Kennedy administration, through the interagency task force, was preparing a budget and legislative program for fiscal 1964.

In the fall of 1962, the Panel on Mental Retardation made its recommendations. President Kennedy was ready to move.

On December 11, 1962, mental health and mental retardation leaders met with Kennedy for the major discussion of both the message to Congress and the bills. The White House staff was represented by Theodore Sorenson, Feldman, and Donohue. The Bureau of the Budget was represented by Daniel Bell, Philip S. Hughes, Hirst Sutton, and March. The Secretary's Office in HEW was represented by Secretary Celebrezze, Wilbur Cohen, Rufus Miles, and Jones. The Public Health Service was represented by Dr. Luther Terry. The Council of Economic Advisors was represented by Walter Heller and Rashi Fein. The executive branch had now completed the design of the president's legislative package.

Cohen briefed Kennedy on the total legislative package in Florida on December 28, 1962.[7] The proposals would represent a major departure in the national approach to mental illness and would involve considerable input of federal resources in the years to come.

Kennedy included in his 1963 "State of the Union" message a new national program in mental health and retardation: "I believe that the abandonment of the mentally ill and the mentally retarded to the grim mercy of custodial institutions too often inflicts on them a needless cruelty which this Nation should not endure." [8] Consequently, he would unfold a new program in a special message to Congress.

Several drafts of the president's message, the first of its kind, were written in the NIMH and edited by Gorman, Feldman, Tarjan, and Brown and reviewed by Cohen, Eunice Shriver, and Sorenson.

Information was leaked to the newspapers that the Kennedy administration planned a massive national offensive against mental illness and mental retardation. In its story on the proposed program, the *Wall Street Journal* noted that the administration's major objective would be to reverse state policy, which stressed long-term isolation of the mentally ill and retarded in big institutions, by a dramatic switch to community centers bankrolled with new federal funds. [9] One of the major channels for this new effort would be the National Institute of Mental Health. For Kennedy, the program had the appeal of raising minimum legislative difficulties, in contrast to such a controversial idea as medical care financed under Social Security. Most of the Mental Retardation Panel's recommendations could be put into effect without new legislation. What was required was merely that bigger budget requests be approved for various health, education, and welfare programs and that some existing appropriation ceilings be raised. The only major new bill required would provide special authority for construction of facilities and for the cost of their operation.

In his special message, Kennedy emphasized that the new knowledge and new drugs developed in recent years had made possible a national mental health program for most of the mentally ill. [10] The program would be designed to treat the mentally ill in their own communities and return them to a useful place in society. He alluded to the fact that the Joint Commission on Mental Illness and Health had pointed out the obsolescence of state mental hospitals. He recommended a national program of community mental health centers.

The president emphasized that, although the concept of the comprehensive community mental health center was new, the separate therapeutic elements to be combined in it were already found in many communities. The centers would focus community resources and provide better community facilities for all aspects of community mental health care. He recommended that $10 million be appropriated to improve care in state mental institutions during the transition to care in local communities. He proposed the appropriation of $66 million for the training of personnel to be employed in mental institutions and community centers.

Kennedy's recommendations for a national program to combat mental retardation were:

1. a new five-year program of project grants to stimulate state and local health departments to plan, initiate, and develop comprehensive maternity and children's health service programs;
2. development of the existing $25 million annual authorization for federal grants for maternal and child health;
3. legislation to develop the present $25 million annual authorization grants for crippled children services over a period of seven years;
4. legislation to assist public welfare in the development of comprehensive plans—i.e., to establish a program of special project grants to the states for financing state review of needs and programs in the field of mental retardation;
5. legislation to assist the states and local communities to construct the facilities their surveys justified and planned—i.e., authorization of matching grants for the construction of public and other nonprofessional facilities, including centers for the comprehensive treatment and care of the mentally retarded;
6. legislation to increase the output of college instructors and classroom teachers for handicapped children.
7. legislation to permit rehabilitation services to be provided to the mentally retarded person for up to eighteen months, subject to the determination of whether or not he had sufficient potential to be rehabilitated vocationally; accompanying legislation establishing new programs to help public and private nonprofessional organizations to construct, equip, and staff rehabilitation centers and workshops, making particular provision for the mentally retarded.
8. legislation to authorize the establishment of centers for research and human development including the training of scientific personnel; and
9. new research authority to the Children's Bureau for research in maternal and child health and crippled children services.[11]

Throughout 1962 the executive branch had been the major source of policy innovation of the community mental health center program and mental retardation program. The congressional committees legitimized the executive initiative in the authorization process of 1963. Congressional committees have a legendary power of life or death over an administration's legislative proposals. Their political power—although sometimes wielded for other than the most rational of reasons—could be steered in directions that were compatible with well-thought-out legislation. Mental health leaders saw the legislative package calling for the creation of community mental health centers as such an instance: they had proposed a rational, nonincremental change from the status quo. But they needed the committees to turn the proposal into law.

Commenting on the power of the committees before he himself was to have a president's experience with them, Woodrow Wilson wrote:

It is evident that there is one principle which runs through every stage of procedure, and which is never disallowed or abrogated—the principle that the Committees shall rule without let or hindrance. And this is a principle of extraordinary formative power. It is the mold of all legislation.[12]

In 1963 two committees were crucial in the molding of the CMHC legislation: the House Interstate and Foreign Commerce Committee and the Senate Committee on Labor and Welfare.

The dynamics of each committee's role system, against the backdrop of its relationship to the president in 1963, shed light on why each committee acted as it did.

## The President's Standing with Congress in 1963

In 1963, John F. Kennedy's honeymoon with Congress was over. The programs of the New Frontier had not been passed. The steel controversy had erupted. Although the president exerted more effort than his predecessors to establish rapport with committees, particularly with their chairmen, his day-by-day congressional relations were difficult. In 1963 he was the executive over an HEW that was proposing a panopoly of health bills: In addition to the mental retardation bill and the mental health bill, it proposed the health professions education bill; revision of hospitals and medical facilities; construction of group practice facilities; specific project grants for improving public health; protecting against environmental hazards; prevention and control of dental diseases; air pollution control; Public Health Service reorganization; health insurance; and maternal and child health care. To Wilbur Cohen and other HEW administrators and the president, "1963 was our weak point; we did not have a hot, effective majority [in Congress]. Our thinking was, if Goldwater runs in 1964, that will be our year!" [13]

In 1963 an innovative president faced a reluctant Congress. Congressmen were especially reluctant to pass any legislation that called for further federal involvement in the nation's health sector, a move opposed by the American Medical Association.

## The Legislative Process

On February 11, Senator Lister Hill introduced S. 755, which was referred to the Committee on Labor and Public Welfare, of which he was chairman. That same day, Congressman Oren Harris introduced H.R. 3688, an identical bill, which was referred to the House Committee on Interstate and

Foreign Commerce, of which he was chairman. On the face of each bill was its purpose: "To provide for assistance in the construction and initial operation of community mental health centers."

Both bills provided that federal matching money would be provided for a period of five years for the construction of community mental health centers including, as a minimum, diagnostic services, inpatient care, outpatient care, and day care for mentally ill persons. Funds would be allotted among the states on the basis of population, the extent of need for community mental health centers, and the financial need of the respective states. The percentage of matching would be roughly similar to that in the Hill-Burton program, with 45 percent as the minimum federal contribution and 75 percent as the maximum. No mention was made of a goal of establishing two thousand community mental health centers.

Both bills also provided for limited federal participation in the operating costs of the centers for approximately four years. For the first fifteen months of the center's operation, the federal grant could not exceed 75 percent of the staffing costs of the center; for the ensuing three years, the federal participation in such costs could not exceed 60 percent, 45 percent, and 30 percent, respectively.

In developing plans for these new services, the president's program called specifically for the participation of all agencies and organizations, both governmental and nongovernmental, which had an interest in mental health. It also stipulated that a state advisory council, made up of representatives of nongovernmental organizations and groups of state agencies, should provide consultation to the state agency developing a state plan.

The one factor certain to be raised in the Congress was the cost of this new legislation. No specific dollar figures had been included in the two bills, since the federal contribution would depend upon just how many states got into the program. For the fiscal year beginning July 1, 1963, the president proposed $190 million for the NIMH, approximately $45 million above the level of expenditures for that year. Rough projections of the cost of the legislation indicated that by 1968 the National Institute of Mental Health budget would have grown to approximately $540 million.

## The Dynamics of the Senate Committee on Labor and Public Welfare

The administration's legislation came before Senator Hill, in two bills—S. 755 (mental illness) and S. 756 (mental retardation)—on February 11, 1963. Hill was the chairman of the Appropriations Committee as well as Committee on Labor and Public Welfare. What he authorized would be funded.

Gorman wanted to ally the interest groups involved in mental retardation with those of the Joint Commission; the retardation groups not only did not yet want such a coalition, they also wanted any new appropriations to be directed primarily to mental retardation programs. Hill did not agree with them. Hence, he considered mental health and mental retardation separately.

Hill and his staff felt that the technology for the centers program existed. They never thought of the program or approached it as a demonstration, which they judged to be inadequate. "We already knew of existing demonstrations through information from NIMH and the interest groups. Moreover, Gorman and Lasker wanted a national program." [14]

## The Senate Hearings

Hill, who often scheduled a hearing with only a one-day or two-days notice, moved quickly. Hearings on S. 755 and S. 756 were held on March 5, 6, and 7. Such a tactic worked against consolidation of opinions by a bill's opponents. Hill kept himself thoroughly informed about the proponents' opinions.

Testimony before the committee contained these themes: For nearly twenty years medical leaders in government and in practice had extensively reappraised the concepts of the care of the mentally ill and mentally retarded. Leaders in other professions had been contributing their knowledge and skills to these studies. The formula grant program of the National Institute of Mental Health for community mental health services had been a beacon encouraging further exploration in those areas since 1946. *Action for Mental Health* pointed up the difficulties of state mental health programs, the acute shortage of personnel, the excessive costs of the current programs, and the need for federal action.

There was no claim that the state and local governments had failed in programming or financing and that, therefore, the federal government should take over. Rather, there was a clear recognition that significantly increased federal funds over a limited period would enable the states and local communities to transfer the care of the mentally ill from state hospitals to local communities.

The strategy of mental health leadership on the staffing grants was that the proposition was one of temporary federal aid phased over the period of greatest financial impact, the initial four years. Ultimate long-term financing would become the responsibility of the community organization— state, local and/or private; thus, each community would be afforded the opportunity, on the one hand, to undertake reasonably prompt comprehensive programs, and, on the other, to have a reasonable lead time as a basis for developing its long-term nonfederal continuing sources of support.

When Senator Frank J. Lausche (D-Ohio) raised the possibility that the CMHC would be permanently subsidized by the federal government, Hill bypassed the question completely.[15]

The testimony reveals the support of the American Medical Association, the American Psychiatric Association, the Conference of Governors, the American Hospital Association, and the National Association of State Mental Health Program Directors and National Association for Mental Health, Inc.

On March 7, 1963, Hill told the president that the centers bill was acceptable in the Senate, but perhaps not to the House. He felt that the president should "jump in" or the program would be weakened.[16] On March 21, 1963, Cohen consolidated the mental health and mental retardation bills at Hill's request.[17] Hill wanted the noncontroversial mental retardation legislation to overshadow the potentially controversial staffing grant provisions of the centers legislation. "Also, many health bills were heating up at the same time. It was easier to bunch them [S. 755 and S. 756] even though we knew the mental retardation group would not like it," according to a committee staff member.[18]

In 1974, Eunice Shriver commented on this mental retardation-mental health strategy:

> It was of great interest at the time and now to have seen the passage of the Community Mental Health Centers Act dependent upon the mental retardation components. The interest for the mental retardation legislation was much more extensive than that for the mental health legislation. The mental health people felt that there was a greater chance for the passage of their legislation if they combined it with the mental retardation legislation.[19]

### The Dynamics of the House Committee on Interstate and Foreign Commerce

The chairman of the committee was Representative Oren Harris, considered one of the most powerful southern House leaders. Although the House Committee on Interstate and Foreign Commerce had authorized the NIMH, Harris had no formal dealings with the mental health leadership in NIMH. The Mental Health Act of 1946 had authorized such broad authority for Felix that he had no reason to report to Harris. From 1955, Felix's primary liaison was with Hill and Fogarty, chairmen of the committees that appropriated funds for NIMH. The community mental health centers legislation necessitated Felix's return to Harris's committee, because it alone could authorize legislation administered under the Public Health Service Act. Gorman, not Felix, would be the primary liaison to Harris, because he was better known to the committee members.

## The Lobbying

Gorman's strategy was, in his own words, to "tangibilitate." [20] He would have the witnesses on the centers legislation in the committee hearings point, as tangible targets, to the archaic state hospitals offering ineffective, inhumane care costly to the states.

Gorman, coordinating the lobbying activity, advised the mental health lobbyists to: (1) know the facts of the situation with which they were dealing; (2) be courteous in all their discussions with congressmen, whether their members happened to agree with them or not; (3) know the opposition and the kinds of arguments being advanced by the opposition; and (4) stick to the facts.

Gorman stressed an agenda that would establish a good line of communication to the representatives, especially the members of the Committee on Interstate and Foreign Commerce. He urged that the interest groups use these tactics:

1. Relate the broad purpose of the legislation to the representative's constituents by providing specific information on the status of the delivery of community mental health services in the representative's district.

2. In the campaign, they should involve local doctors on whom congressmen relied for advice in health matters. (The lobbyists were to remind the doctors of two facts: the president's message stressed the role of the private physician in treating his own patients in the proposed community mental health centers; and the AMA supported multiple-source financing for community mental health services and accepted the need to expand this financing.

3. Representatives of the local mental health associations, civic organizations, and the medical society either should come to see their congressmen in Washington or back in their districts.

4. If the bill became bottled up in the Interstate and Foreign Commerce Committee, they were to devote particular attention to the thirty-three members of that committee. If a good line of communication was established, their telegrams might help in turning the tide. Telegrams would be of little use if the congressmen had not been educated previously on the issue.

5. If congressmen said that they were for the program but that the budget deficit precluded this new expense, they were to respond with the

economic argument developed by Fein and adopted by the president: mental illness and mental retardation yearly cost the taxpayers $2.4 billion in direct public outlays, with indirect public outlays (welfare costs and the waste of human resources) running even higher.[21]

Both committee members and the staffs relied on the judgment of HEW to provide feasible alternatives. The staff of the House Committee on Interstate and Foreign Commerce was aware that there were positive demonstrable results of patient care in the community, in contrast to warehousing of the patients in state mental hospitals. The staff and the members thought that mental health centers should be available to virtually everyone. They were familiar with the Hill-Burton type of funding for the construction of the centers. They were also well aware that should they authorize the CMHC program, it would be fully funded by Fogarty on Appropriations—if past successes in funding NIH and NIMH were to continue. They knew that the Joint Commission and the president's message had alerted the electorate.[22]

The AMA position also seemed clear to them. The AMA program, approved by its Board of Trustees and House of Delegates in the summer of 1962, concurred with President Kennedy's stress on comprehensive care of mental patients at the community level rather than in large, remote state institutions. The AMA "Statement of Principles on Mental Health" and on the president's legislative package supported matching grants made to the states by the federal government for construction of community mental health facilities.

On March 1, 1963, Dr. Gerald D. Dorman, an AMA trustee, told the Ninth Annual Conference of State Mental Health Representatives: "I am hopeful that this, the Kennedy's Administration mental health program, marks the beginning of a truly non-partisan, non-political attack on mental illness." [23] Another point of agreement was encompassed in the president's message, Dorman said, in that Kennedy recommended that services provided by the community centers should be financed through individual fees for service, individual and group insurance, other third-party payments, voluntary and private contributions, and state and local aid.

*The House Hearings*

On February 11, 1963, Harris had introduced H.H. 3688 and H.R. 3689 on behalf of the administration to establish comprehensive community health centers, and to construct research centers and facilities for the mentally retarded. Between March 26 and 28, 1963, Representative Kenneth A. Roberts (D-Ala.), chairman of the Subcommittee on Public Health and Safety of the Committee on Interstate and Foreign Commerce, conducted hearings on both bills, with Harris participating. The committee members considered both bills together, feeling that they dealt with an interrelated national mental health program. It also seems that the members, especially Harris (Jones in the administration and Gorman agreeing), were aware that allying the mental health interest groups with those interested in mental retardation around the same bill would help to defuse a negative reaction on the staffing grant provisions from Congress.

**The Administration's Presentation.** Secretary Celebrezze outlined the president's legislative package, although the burden of the substantive testimony on the community mental health center program fell to his special assistant, "Bo" Jones. Wilbur Cohen, assistant secretary for legislation, handled the testimony on the mental retardation program.

Jones' testimony made several critical points:

1. Special legislation was required for construction and initial staffing of the centers because the necessary authorization of funds exclusively for service program did not exist under the Public Health Services Act.

2. The matching formula for the construction grants used the pattern of the Hill-Burton program, but at a higher level (45 to 75 percent versus 33⅓ to 66⅔ percent), to provide an additional stimulus to communities and states to develop the center facilities. This part of the program would be coordinated through the Federal Hospital Council, the statutory advisory council for the Hill-Burton program.

3. Because participation by the federal government would decrease 75 to 60, to 45 to 30 percent in the ensuing four years after construction of the centers, the cost of operating a center would be met by the traditional financing patterns for the care of the physically ill in a community. The administration of the staffing grants would be in the Public Health Service.

Jones concluded:

> So what we are really advocating, Mr. Chairman, is, in a sense, removing the care of the mentally ill from complete, almost complete, responsibility of the state through tax funds and direct operations in these isolated large state mental institutions, and putting this care back in the community to be financed and supported and operated through the traditional patterns of medical care to which we have become accustomed in this country. This means providing for the mentally ill in precisely the same pattern that we provide for physically ill.
>
> But we think that some grant-in-aid support of the kind envisioned in this proposal will be important to encourage and to stimulate communities to develop the comprehensive center that will make possible caring for the emotionally disturbed, the mentally ill, and to assist in preventing mental illness through training of ministers, of social work-

ers, of teachers, of police officers, of juvenile court representation in the community in order that mental health will be promoted.

That is the concept of the operating support for a limited period of years.[24]

The history of NIMH and its programmatic accomplishments in research, training, and services were introduced into the record. Congressman Ancher Nelson (R-Minn.) suggested that it might be difficult to withdraw the proposed staffing support at the end of the proposed four-year period. Jones responded that the decreasing authorities during the four years were designed to prepare state and local communities for the full assumption of staffing costs at the end of the program. Paul Rogers (D-Fla.) referred to the current shortage of medical manpower and questioned the wisdom of providing facilities without assuring sources of staff and personnel. He agreed with Jones that the enactment of H.R. 12, which dealt with the training of certain types of personnel, would alleviate this problem.[25]

Cohen's task was to explain the mental retardation aspects of the bill and also to ensure adequate care of, and research on, the mentally retarded as desired by retardation advocates. He did so by delineating mental retardation and mental illness as separate health problems: mental retardation involved intellectual defects frequently present at birth or in early childhood; mental illness included problems of personality and behavior disorders often manifested in young and older adults after a period of relatively normal development. He argued that separating categorical earmarked funds for mental retardation efforts from the mental health bill would assure that there would not be divisions in the community about federal funds, but that different groups interested in each of these problems in the local community would give full support and attention to their problem.[26]

The mental retardation bill (H.R. 3689) would provide ten regional research centers to research the problems of mental retardation and to train persons to work with the mentally retarded and the construction of facilities for the mentally retarded. There were no staffing provisions in H.R. 3689. The description of HEW programs in the mental retardation field was inserted into the record.[27] Thus, in meeting the interests of the mental retardation advocates, Cohen helped to keep the coalition together.

**The States' Presentation.** Governor Frank G. Clement of Tennessee reminded the committee members of the governors' support for the community mental health center program. He said it was reasonable from a therapeutic and economic standpoint, and consistent with the findings of the Joint Commission's report. The governors had previously advocated such a program at their Conference on Mental Health on November 10,

1961. Governor Clement produced written supportive statements of many of the governors, especially from the large states.[28]

Dr. V. Terrel Davis, vice-president of the National Association of State Mental Health Program Directors, testified that the consensus of his group was that the centers program reflected the trends around community services. At their meeting in September 1963, the directors agreed that their main problem was inadequate funds; the large state hospitals had to be improved to take care of the overcrowding, short staffing, and increasingly complex administration. In response to the committee's questions on the current percentage of state budgets devoted to mental health and mental retardation, Davis produced tables of estimated per capita expenditures for a ten-year period. In effect, he documented the fiscal efforts of the states. Despite their expenditures, the states required federal financial assistance.[29]

**The Testimony of the Mental Health Professionals.** Dr. Jack R. Ewalt, director of the Joint Commission on Mental Illness and Health, followed the governor's testimony. On behalf of his colleagues on the commission and of the organizations they represented, he supported the federal stimulation of the community mental health centers program. The act, he noted, was not a crash program but a well-planned one, based on existing technology.[30] Ewalt's testimony was crucial, since it created the political myth that the Joint Commission supported a bill designed to direct the major federal effort into the community and not into the state mental hospital system. Ewalt had argued within the commission that the major recommendation should be emphasis on community mental health programs. The major recommendation of the commission was that major federal investment should be in the state system. Ewalt's testimony was an excellent finesse by the mental health leadership.

Dr. Francis J. Braceland reported on behalf of the American Psychiatric Association. The return of the patient to the community was the next phase in the mission the mental health leadership had set out upon seventeen years before (the 1946 Mental Health Act) with the Congress's blessing. The bill was timely, because there was a growing appreciation of the need for more community clinics, guidance centers, and outpatient, as well as inpatient, facilities.[31]

The American Hospital Association, American Public Health Association, the AFL-CIO, and pharmaceutical interests, as well as others, testified in favor of the bill (H.R. 3688).[32]

**The Testimony of the AMA.** In 1963, the American Medical Association had one of the most effective and efficient lobbying organizations in Washington. Lobbyists were assigned to each congressman and could contact virtually every member of the House in a few hours.[33]

The testimony of the AMA seemed to support the bill. However, a careful analysis of the testimony of its witness, Dr. Lindsay E. Beaton, a psychiatrist, and Dr. Charles L. Hudson, a member of the AMA Board of Trustees, reveals a disagreement between factions on the organization's position on the staffing grant provisions:

> The AMA Statement of Principles on Mental Health recognizes the national shortage of mental health facilities and services and urges that those needs be met at the community level. To encourage this community responsibility, H.R. 3688 not only proposed to provide matching funds for the construction of the facility, but also funds to subsidize a substantial part of the cost of staffing the activity during its initial years.
>
> Whether the Federal Government should provide a part of the funds for staffing is a question that we cannot resolve within the limited time we have had to consider the measure. One viewpoint holds that such Federal financial assistance during the early years will enable the community mental health center to undertake a properly staffed program from the start. Further, that within a short period of time, the influx of patients and the probable transfer of state funds from other institutional facilities will make continued Federal financing support unnecessary. And, finally, that many communities do not have the resources to pay the initial staffing costs needed to insure a successful program. This opinion is conditioned upon the four-year limitation placed on Federal participation.
>
> A second point of view maintains that the Federal participation under the bill should be limited to the construction costs of the community mental health center. It is urged that once a center has been constructed, the community should assume the remaining responsibility. This viewpoint reflects the feeling that once reliance is placed on Federal subsidy for staffing, the role of the Federal Government as a provider of funds will not easily be terminated.[34]

Why did the AMA present two viewpoints? Paragraph two reflected the position of the psychiatrists of the AMA's Council on Mental Health. They had negotiated this plank in the AMA Statement of Principles on Mental Health:

> In terms of tax dollars, responsibility for the support and development of community health programs must be shared by local, state and Federal agencies. In such programs, the apportionment of funds will vary depending on the wealth and industrial tax base of communities and states involved.[35]

Paragraph three reflected the lack of a position by the AMA Board of Trustees in March 1963.

## Senate Action

The Senate Committee on Labor and Public Welfare met in executive session Tuesday morning (May 21, 1963) to consider S. 755-756. The committee reported favorably on the mental health and mental retardation titles and added a new title desired by Senator Edward Kennedy and Senator Hill on the training of teachers of the mentally retarded and other handicapped children.

## The AMA-GOP Entente

The AMA's Mental Health Council had testified in favor of the bill. On June 19, 1963, the AMA House of Delegates repudiated the Council on Mental Health by adopting a motion at its Atlantic City meeting disapproving of "the concept of Federal funds for staffing mental health institutions." The organization also said it had "serious misgivings" on federal grants for bricks-and-mortar for mental health centers.[36] Through this action of the House of Delegates, the Council on Legislative Activities and the Board of Trustees had maneuvered to protect the economic interests of its members and to defeat the "liberal" drift of the Council on Mental Health. The council had served as the AMA beachhead for the mental health leadership. The staffing grant controversy represented a fight by the ultraconservative part of AMA against federal support of doctors' salaries at the state and local level; it was part of the "socialized medicine" furor. The doctors stated that they were fighting for a principle and believed that if they won, they would have blocked "socialized medicine" in an important move.

Immediately after the AMA's vote against the staffing provision, the lobbyists had personally contacted every member of the House. But on the same day as the action of the House of Delegates, Roberts's subcommittee had voted for the bill, including the initial staffing program. Interstate and Foreign Commerce chairman Harris had indicated his support for the initial staffing program, a signal to Roberts that the full committee supported his work. Coupled with Harris's support was the fact that Republican members of the subcommittee had voted for the bills.[37]

After the subcommittee's vote, the House Republican Policy Committee decided to make a partisan stand against the staffing provisions of President Kennedy's mental health-mental retardation measure.[38] The GOP and the AMA were philosophically in agreement on health measures. The president's position with Congress was weak. GOP opposition could deprive the president of at least total success on these domestic measures of special importance to him.

## The Season of Bargaining

With the opposition of the GOP members of his committee, Chairman Harris faced a close vote. On June 27, the full committee referred the administration's bill back to Roberts's health subcommittee for the technical reason that the Senate had added a new section to S. 1576, not in the House bill, which dealt with the training of teachers for the mentally retarded. Harris also indicated that some committee members felt that more information should be developed on the House bill before he reported it to the floor for a vote.

On June 28, 1963, Dr. F. J. L. Blasingame, on behalf of the AMA, formally notified Roberts on his request: "The American Medical Association supports the provision of S. 1576 which pertains to the construction of facilities. The Association, however, is opposed to the Federal participation in the financing of the cost of initial staffing of community mental health centers." [39]

In late June, Representative Paul Rogers proposed that the administration bargain by lowering the price of the staffing grants, a proposition to which Harris agreed. NIMH, in collaboration with the HEW Secretary's Office, reduced the number of psychiatrists, psychologists, social workers, health educators, and occupational therapists as part of the staffing pattern, thereby lowering the costs. The committee itself considered various construction and staffing alternatives.

Between July 10 and 12, 1963, Roberts conducted special hearings on the staffing provisions. Harris did not yet want to propose a compromise with the Republicans. HEW Medical Affairs Assistant Jones, PHS Surgeon General Terry, and NIMH Director Felix, testifying on July 10, argued that federal support for initial staffing would provide "seed" money to stimulate local responsibility.

By July 12, Jones expressed to Felix the view that there was no outside hope for passage of the staffing grants.[40] The National Association of State Mental Health Program Directors put on four physician witnesses "from the firing line." These practitioners had the facts, and they used them. The congressmen treated them with respect; not one opposed their testimony. However, Harris's remark, "I only wish that every member of this Committee could have heard this," [41] indicates that some members of the committee were not present because they had already made their decision in opposition.

Roberts had the votes to report the bill out favorably to the full committee, but Harris anticipated a solid Republican vote against staffing and had to hold all Democrats in line. Following the executive session during the week of July 15, Roberts reported favorably S. 1576 (as passed by the Senate) with a number of amendments.

Throughout July and early August, the mental health lobbyists attempted to rally support for the legislation. People of high standing and influence in business contacted the members of the House Committee on Interstate and Foreign Commerce personally. On July 31, 1963, the National Association of Counties unanimously supported a four-year construction and eight-year staffing program—but to no avail.

On August 14, the House Committee on Interstate and Foreign Commerce ordered S. 1576 reported to the House floor. The provisions for federal assistance to fight retardation (Title I) came through unscathed, with congressmen reporting heavy popular pressure for those provisions.

The mental health centers part of the bill (Title II), however, was a shrunken bill. In a vote closely adhering to party lines, the House committee reduced the money provisions 70 percent below the Senate-passed version: a $238 million authorization versus a $847 million Senate authorization. The committee eliminated federal funds for staffing in the formative years. Harris's estimate of the closeness of the vote had been accurate:

FOR THE MOTION
(against staffing)

*Three Democrats*
John Bell Williams (Miss.)
W. R. Hull, Jr. (Mo.)
Lionel Van Deerlin (Calif.)

*Twelve Republicans*
John B. Bennett (Mich.)
William L. Springer (Ill.)
J. Arthur Younger (Calif.)
Milton W. Glenn (N.J.)
Samuel L. Devine (Ohio)
Ancher Nelson (Minn.)
Hastings Keith (Mass.)
Willard S. Curtin (Penn.)

AGAINST THE MOTION
(for staffing)

*Twelve Democrats*
Oren Harris (Ark.)
Kenneth Roberts (Ala.)
Walter Rogers (Tex.)
Samuel N. Friedel (Md.)
Torbert H. McDonald (Mass.)
George M. Rhodes (Penn.)
Leo W. O'Brien (N.Y.)
John E. Moss (Calif.)
John D. Dingell (Mich.)
Paul G. Rogers (Fla.)
Dan Rostenkowski (Ill.)
Gillis W. Long (La.)

Abner W. Sibal (Conn.)
Glenn Cunningham (Neb.)
James T. Broyhill (N.C.)
Donald G. Brotzman (Colo.)

*GOP*
*No Republicans*

TOTAL    15

TOTAL    12

NOT PRESENT

*One Republican*
Paul F. Schenck (Ohio)

*Five Democrats*
Harley O. Staggers (W.Va.)
John Jarman (Okla.)
Robert W. Hemphil (S.C.)
James C. Healey (N.Y.)
Horace R. Kornegay (N.C.)

(Van Deerlin was FOR staffing but voted with the majority in a parliamentary maneuver to provide for reconsideration of the motion the next day if the strategists so deemed.) [42]

After the staffing vote on Tuesday, Harris met privately the same night with his colleagues, during which time he seems to have deflated the AMA arguments. He realized that he could swing the vote the next day in favor of the staffing provisions, but knew that he would risk a floor fight, a risk that, as chairman, he would rather not take. It was also clear that the White House did not want to expend any more political capital on a floor fight. Such a fight could jeopardize the whole bill, especially the mental retardation section; furthermore, the construction provisions of Title II did represent at least a foot in the door. The staffing grant provisions were not timely but would be in the future.

Harris's committee had functioned as the mediator between the mental health leadership and the AMA. Their opposing positions had to be compromised before being acceptable to the majority of the Congress and the medical profession. As Congressman Abner W. Sibal (R-Conn.) later stated: "It [the centers legislation] has been cut down to the smallest common denominator possible." [43]

In August and September, the major mental health lobbies—the National Association for Mental Health, Inc., the National Association of State Mental Health Program Directors, and the Committee Against Mental Illness—flooded congressmen with mail to show that there was ground swell of opinion in favor of the mental health legislation so that should a prostaffing amendment from the House floor be offered, it might be accepted. Also, they attempted to stimulate newspaper comment expressing concern about congressional irresponsibility and calling upon the president for renewed leadership in support of his mental health program. Local members of these organizations wired their congressman urging them to restore the cuts in S. 1576, especially the staffing cut. They also sent telegrams to President Kennedy urging him to give outspoken leadership and to Senator Lister Hill thanking him for his leadership.[44]

The response of the House was decisive and clear. On September 10, 1963, the full House considered the Mental Retardation Facilities and Community Mental Health Centers Construction Act of 1963. The House leadership adhered to the tradition of permitting the committee chairman (Harris) and the ranking minority member (Springer) to organize and administer the discussion of the committee-reported bill when it was debated. Such a procedure acknowledges the member's primacy within his party's contingent delegation on the committee, and it occurs even though the chairman may actually object to the contents of a bill he defends. Neither Harris nor Roberts agreed with the full committee's negative vote on staffing, but they defended the amended bill reported unanimously from the committee.

Harris argued that the majority of his committee had deleted the staffing provision because it was so controversial and thereby the committee did not set a new federal precedent. The majority felt that the states could provide staffing. He warned his fellow House members:

When the Committee made that decision, as is usual, my position is to stay with the Committee on it, and I am supporting the action of the Committee and will oppose any effort or any attempt to offer amendments today to reestablish a program for staffing of personnel for these centers.[45]

Other members of the House mentioned that they had received mail from many constituents, who were authorities in the field, indicating that the question of staffing of the centers was the heart of the bill. It was obvious to both laymen and professionals in the mental health field that the need for services at the local level far outweighed the ability of the local community to pay for them. William L. Springer (R-Ill.) responded that he did not believe it would be possible for Congress to deny staffing in other programs if the members approved staffing in this bill.[46]

Alabama Democrat Kenneth Roberts expressed his feeling that this was a piece of landmark legislation, but he added:

I was frankly not happy about cutting the staffing, because I believe that this is the place where we may or may not get the results we would have gotten had the Federal Government gone in for a limited period of time and helped out with the staffing problem.[47]

George M. Rhodes, a member of Roberts's subcommittee, was even more direct:

> The staffing provision has widespread national support and the endorsement of many local groups interested in this problem. . . . The overwhelming weight of professional opinion is recorded in the testimony on this legislation in strong support of the initial staffing fund. . . .
> A political decision later resulted in the A.M.A.'s opposition to this provision. This body should not fail to note that the competent professionals, the experts on mental health, within the A.M.A., recommended otherwise. It is unfortunate that the majority of the Committee on Interstate and Foreign Commerce chose to follow the political views of the A.M.A. leadership rather than the professional views of the A.M.A.'s own expert body in this field.[48]

Thus, for the record, Rhodes had described the detrimental pressure of the AMA leadership. Others agreed. Such remarks would occur frequently in the next two years, not only in relation to this bill, but to other health measures. The stage was being set—if not the staffing grants this time, then very soon. No amendment for staffing was presented on September 10, 1963. The floor would defer to the authority of Harris.

Nelson referred to the fact that the bill represented a program of federal "seed" money, allowing the prime responsibility to rest with the states and communities.[49] May pointed out, however, that mental illness was a national problem and did not belong exclusively to the states.

Rogers presented a cost-benefit argument in favor of the community mental health approach as an alternative to state hospitals. Other members endorsed his argument. The talents and skills of the mentally ill should not be lost to society.[50]

William Ryan of New York emphasized that support for the community centers project came from the director of the National Institute of Mental Health, Dr. Robert M. Felix.[51] Halperin introduced the data showing the inability of state mental hospitals to rehabilitate the mentally disabled. He contrasted Americans' inadequate national response with the national programs and successes of Denmark and Sweden. Claude Pepper (D-Tenn.), who had been a key senator in the passage of Public Law 487 of the Seventy-ninth Congress authorizing the establishment of NIMH, strongly supported the enactment of the centers legislation as consistent with the growth toward a national mental health program.

Harris firmly, but not finally, committed himself and his fellow House conferees prior to the vote to stand by the House version of the bill, as reported by the Committee, and specifically not to grant money for the initial staffing of the centers. Springer recommended that the legislation should pass because it was "in the public interest." The vote was then taken: yeas, 335; nays, 18; not voting, 80. The bill then went to conference.

The hearings before the authorizing committees had highlighted the respective committee role systems. In fact, the personal commitments, values, and constituency pressures were reflected in the behavior of committee members once hearings were underway and, in the case of the Committee on Interstate and Foreign Commerce, in their decision to hold second hearings. The first set of hearings before the House committee and Hill's Senate committee resulted in sufficient publicity to encourage groups, especially the AMA, to pressure for changes in each member's position. The hearings had functioned as a means to assess opposition to the proposal, especially the staffing grant provisions.

## The Senate-House Conference

Prior to the conference, Cohen recommended to Feldman that, despite House resistance to restoring any part of staffing grant provisions, the administration should give strong support to some compromise position on that provision. He suggested that the percentage figures in the Senate bill (75, 60, 45, and 30) could be reduced somewhat and the duration of grant assistance to any project might be reduced by a year if necessary. However, if the House was to remain adamant in its opposition to the whole concept, nothing would be gained by a bargain offer.[52]

The mental health lobby had decided to renew the pressure on the House. On September 25, thirty physicians from twenty states sent telegrams to nine congressmen who were the House members of the joint committee on S. 1576. The doctors favored temporary operational support of the centers.[53]

In an unprecedented action, the Fifteenth Mental Hospital Institute passed a resolution on September 26, urging the House-Senate conferees to restore to S. 1576 provisions for temporary federal assistance for operation of the comprehensive rapid treatment mental health centers to be built under other sections of the bill. The Mental Hospital Institute consisted of over five hundred physicians, nurses, mental hospital superintendents, business administrators, state mental health directors, psychologists, social workers, chaplains, and many other mental hospital personnel. The resolution, which was wired to all congressmen on the joint conference committee, was as follows:

*BE IT RESOLVED THAT:* This institute go on record as urging the Senate and House conference committee to restore support for the initial staffing of the community mental health centers contemplated by S. 1576.

It is our conviction that such temporary operational support is absolutely essential to getting the community centers launched and firmly established in the community.

We who have labored so long in mental hospitals under the handicaps of personnel shortages know that buildings alone are not enough. It will be the services provided that count.

Once the centers are operationally underway, they can be paid for in local communities like other medical facilities. But they need this initial help to establish their roots in the communities of our Nation. A great opportunity is at hand to bring the mentally ill back into the mainstream of medicine. We urge you not to allow this bill to pass without some initial support for operational services in the centers.[54]

On October 16, 1963, Dr. V. Terrell Davis told members of the National Association of State Mental Health Program Directors to notify the House-Senate conferees that the states wanted the initial staffing provision.[55] The lobbying activity was intense but, as events inside the conference indicate, not successful.

In the conference on October 1, 1963, Title I of the Mental Retardation-Mental Health bill, relating to mental retardation, was agreed upon. However, for Title II b, all of the House Democratic members, led by Harris, said "no staffing" for mental health centers. This was a surprise, because the administration expected a compromise along the lines suggested by Cohen, and the Senate Republican members (particularly New York Senator Jacob Javits) wanted a compromise.[56] The conference was deadlocked. The next meeting was scheduled for October 8, but there was to be no compromise.

Representative J. Arthur Younger (R-Calif.), a substitute for conferee Schenck, wrote to a constituent on October 4, 1963:

We will not agree to the staffing provision and if they were to put that back in the conference report, the entire bill would be defeated in the House. We feel it is far more important to get the construction programs underway rather than being concerned with the staffing of the clinics at the present time.[57]

The administration knew that Dr. Robbins of Arkansas (a long-time personal friend and political supporter of Harris) was behind Harris's position. Other doctors of the same persuasion (conservative) were similarly behind the other Democrats on the committee. Dr. Stafford L. Warren, special assistant to the president for mental retardation, suggested to the president that he propose to Harris the elimination of doctors' salaries in exchange for the provision of salaries for the support of paramedical personnel (nurses, therapists, social workers, etc.) and/or provision for demonstration programs including salaries for the same.[58] Jones advised that the president should not ask a friend (Harris) that which Harris felt he could not do.[59]

On Thursday, October 17, the conferees met for two hours. Prior to the meeting, the National Association for Mental Health advised the two chairmen that 247 congressmen would support a bill with staffing.[60] House leaders are not always sold on "outside-the-family" polls, however. They feel that their fellow congressmen are inclined to agree with constituent queries, but complex changes in a bill prior to a second vote always give a man an excuse for "changing position." Harris certainly felt the same, since he testified later to the full House and repudiated the NAMH poll.[61]

The conferees could not agree that the bill would pass the House with an "initial staffing" provision in it (an extra $169 million). Virtually all conferees acknowledged the value of staffing money to the states, but the majority of House conferees were reluctant to jeopardize the bill by restoring the staffing provision. Consequently, the Senate-House conferees approved S. 1576 without provisions for "initial staffing." They compromised on the total cost for the approved programs: $91 million more than the House-passed bill; $521 million less than the Senate-passed bill.

The final total was $329 million: $179 million for the retardation programs and $150 million for the mental health centers.

## Passage of the Bill

On October 21, 1963, Hill submitted to the Senate the report of the Committee of Conference. He stated that although the staffing provisions were not restored, it was the intent of the conferees that, in addition to S. 1576, the Public Health Service use its existing authorities and resources for the establishment and temporary operation of the centers. The Senate agreed to the report.[62]

On the same day, Harris reported to the House that the House conferees had successfully maintained the position of the House on staffing and compromised on the funding of the mental retardation programs. Nonetheless, the conferees had accepted a new concept in dealing with the mentally ill in this country, never before put into operation on a national scale. Although they spoke of local mental health centers, they did not delineate an objective of covering the country with two thousand centers as discussed in the president's task force.

I believe we will have an opportunity to watch this program develop. And if it does appear it cannot get off the ground without additional psychiatrists, psychologists and nurses trained in this field, I hope to offer a bill later on to accomplish these purposes. . . .

Although since the beginning of the attack on this problem, mental illness has been subject to state socialized medicine, this bill, the Conference Bill, will utilize and encourage private medicine to make its best contribution.[63]

Rhodes reiterated his positive position on the staffing provision. He did not agree that funds for initial staffing were entirely a state or local responsibility or that the program could not be justified because of the budgetary problem.[64]

The question was taken. The conference bill passed—yeas, 296; nays, 4; not voting, 123. President Kennedy signed Public Law 88-164, the Community Mental Health Centers Act, on October 31, 1963.

## A Nonincremental Process

The congressional allies of the mental health leaders had provided a new, innovative policy through the traditional congressional committee process without inconsequential debate and compromise. The policy was nonincremental. The mental health leaders had recommended a *national* community mental health care system, a totally new concept.

Initiated on the presidential level and steered through committee levels by the skill of the pro-mental-health leadership in Congress, the concept was accepted by the Congress. The mental health partisans oriented the public and their elected representatives to accept the concept of community care. The mental health elite collaborated to push the community mental health center program through committee processes.

The funding of mental health facilities, but not of staffing, in the final outcome in 1963 was not a critical setback to the leadership. The construction of the facilities would necessitate staffing in the near future. Congressmen would not leave facilities empty. Felix, Yolles, Atwell, Cohen, Hill, Harris, Fogarty, and Kennedy knew this political reality. The construction of the centers presupposed the staffing as justifiable congressional action. The mental health entrepreneurs had taken the king with a pawn. The AMA's and the GOP Policy Committee's victory in 1963 was to prove a Pyrrhic one.

# Notes

1. Interview with Mike Gorman, 24 March 1972.
2. Interview with Dr. George Tarjan, 29 July 1972.
3. Gorman.
4. Tarjan.
5. Dr. Robert Felix, *Hearings before U.S. Senate Subcommittee of the Committee on Appropriations-Department of Labor and HEW Appropriations for 1963,* 10 April 1962, pp. 8-9.
6. Ibid.
7. Interview with Wilbur Cohen, 14 May 1972.
8. John F. Kennedy, "State of the Union," 14 January 1963.
9. Jonathan Spivak, "Fighting Mental Ills," *The Wall Street Journal,* 15 January 1963.
10. John F. Kennedy, "Special Message on Mental Illness and Mental Retardation," 5 February 1963.
11. Ibid.
12. Woodrow Wilson, *Congressional Government* (New York: Maridian Edition, 1956), p. 66.
13. Cohen.
14. Interview with Mr. Robert Barclay, staffer to Senate Committee on Labor and Public Welfare, June 1972.
15. Ibid.
16. Notes on a conversation between Mr. Atwell and Mr. Van Stadden regarding BOB, 7 March 1963.
17. Memo to Secretary from Wilbur Cohen, 19 March 1963. Files on 88-164, Office of the General Counsel, HEW.
18. Barclay.
19. From Eunice K. Shriver to Henry A. Foley, 3 January 1974.
20. Gorman.
21. Gorman prepared this strategy in a statement, "How Mental Health Associations Can Rally Support for the President's Mental Health Program," distributed in memorandum from Philip E. Ryan, executive director of National Association for Mental Health, Inc., to executive directors, NAMH Divisions.
22. Interview with Mr. James Menger, 7 June 1972; Barclay.
23. News Release from the American Medical Association, 1 March 1962.
24. *Hearings* before a Subcommittee of the Committee on Interstate and Foreign Commerce, House of Representatives, 26, 27, and 28 March 1963, p. 97.
25. Ibid., pp. 99-107.

26. Cohen.

27. *Hearings,* pp. 107-46.

28. Ibid., pp. 147-68.

29. Ibid., pp. 215-23.

30. Ibid., pp. 239-43.

31. Ibid., pp. 243-53.

32. Ibid.

33. Menger.

34. *Hearings,* pp. 339-40.

35. Ibid., p. 335.

36. Memorandum: "Recent Action by A.M.A. House of Delegates on Community Mental Health Center Bill" (June 19, 1963—Atlantic City) from National Association State Mental Health Program Directors.

37. "The Blue Sheet," *Drug Research Reports* (Washington, D.C.), 10 July 1963.

38. Ibid., p. 2.

39. From F. J. L. Blasingame, M.D., American Medical Association, to Honorable Kenneth A. Roberts, Chairman 28 June 1963.

40. Message from Jones to Felix typed by LKR.

41. Quoted by Harry C. Schnibbe in "Memo to All State Directors," 12 July 1963, in Information, National Association State Mental Health Program Directors.

42. Memorandum, 6 September 1963, from Harry C. Schnibbe to Phil Ryan, NAMH. Subject: House Committee Vote on the Staffing Provision. With statement, "A Congressman who was present told me it was as follows." Verified by "Mental Bill Stripped," *Washington Report on the Medical Sciences,* 19 August 1963.

43. *Congressional Record,* 10 September 1963, p. 15803.

44. Memo to Max Silverstein from Philip E. Ryan, Executive Director, The National Association for Mental Health, Inc., 4 September 1963.

45. *Congressional Record,* 10 September 1963, p. 15788.

46. Ibid., p. 15794.

47. Ibid., p. 15798.

48. Ibid., p. 15801.

49. Ibid., pp. 15800-01.

50. Ibid., p. 15806.

51. Ibid., p. 15807.

52. Memorandum for Honorable Myer Feldman. Subject: S. 1576—Conference Committee. From Wilbur J. Cohen, 18 September 1963, p. 4.

53. "Doctors Favor Temporary Operation Support of Centers," *Information National State Mental Health Program Directors,* 26 September 1963.

54. "Mental Health Institute Backs Operational Support for Rapid Treatment Centers," *Information National Association State Mental Health Program Directors.*

55. Memorandum from V. Terrel Davis, president, from National Association State Mental Health Program directors, 16 October 1963.

56. "Information Memorandum for the President—Urgent." From Stafford L. Warren, M.D., Special Assistant to the President for Mental Retardation, 2 October 1963.

57. To Mr. Robert H. Klein, from J. Arthur Younger, M.D., 11th District, California, 4 October 1963.

58. Warren.

59. Interview with Jones, 3 April 1972.

60. "Memorandum to all State Mental Health Directors," *Information National Association State Mental Health Program Directors,* 10 October 1963.

61. *Congressional Record,* 21 October 1963, p. 18968.

62. Ibid., p. 18851.

63. Ibid., p. 18969.

64. Ibid., p. 18970.

## Bibliography

*Books*

Binkley, Wilfred E. *President and Congress.* New York: Vintage Books, 1962.

Clapp, Charles L. *The Congressman, His Work As He Sees It.* Washington, D.C.: The Brookings Institution, 1963.

Morrow, William L. *Congressional Committees.* New York: Charles Scribner's & Sons, 1969.

Wilson, Woodrow. *Congressional Government.* New York: Maridian Edition, 1956.

*Articles, Letters, Memoranda*

Spivak, Jonathan. "Fighting Mental Ills." *The Wall Street Journal,* 15 January 1963.

News Release from the American Medical Association, 1 March 1962.

"The Blue Sheet." *Drug Research Reports.* Washington, D.C., 10 July 1963.

From F. J. L. Blasingame, M.D., American Medical Association, to Honorable Kenneth A. Roberts, Chairman, 28 June 1963.

From J. Arthur Younger, M.D. 11th District, California, to Mr. Robert H. Klein, 4 October 1963.

From Eunice K. Shriver to Henry A. Foley, 3 January 1974.

From Jones to Felix, typed by LKR, July 1963.

"County Officials Support Federal Program for Rapid Treatment Centers." *Information National Association State Mental Health Program Directors,* 1 August 1963.

Memo to Max Silverstein from Philip E. Ryan, Executive Director, 4 September 1963, *The National Association for Mental Health, Inc.*

Memorandum 6 September 1963 from Harry C. Schnibbe to Phil Ryan, NAMH. Subject: House Committee Vote on the Staffing Provision. With statement "A Congressman who was present told me it was as follows." Verified by "Mental Bill Stripped." *Washington Report on the Medical Sciences,* 19 August 1963.

Memorandum for Honorable Myer Feldman. Subject: S. 1576—Conference Committee. From Wilbur J. Cohen, 18 September 1963, p. 4.

"Doctors Favor Temporary Operation Support of Centers." *Information National State Mental Health Program Directors,* 26 September 1963.

"Information Memorandum for the President—Urgent." From Stafford L. Warren, M.D., Special Assistant to the President for Mental Retardation, 2 October 1963.

"Memorandum to all State Mental Health Directors." *Information National Association State Mental Health Program Directors,* 10 October 1963.

Memorandum from V. Terrel Davis, President, National Association State Mental Health Program Directors, 16 October 1963.

Notes typed by LKR on 12 December 1962 for George Van Stadden, NIMH Files.

Notes on a conversation between Mr. Atwell and Mr. Van Stadden regarding BOB, 7 March 1963.

Memo to Secretary from Wilbur Cohen, 19 March 1963, Files on 88-164, Office of the General Counsel, HEW.

Memorandum: "Recent Action by A.M.A. House of Delegates on Community Mental Health Center Bill" (19 June 1963—Atlantic City) from National Association State Mental Health Program Directors.

"Notes on a Call from Dr. Stewart," 25 June 1963, NIMH Files.

"Notes, 1 July 1963," NIMH Director, NIMH Files.

Quoted by Harry C. Schnibbe in "Memo to All State Directors," 12 July 1963, in Information National Association State Mental Health Program Directors.

*Addresses*

Kennedy, John F. "State of the Union," 14 January 1963.
Kennedy, John F. "Special Message on Mental Illness and Mental Retardation," 5 February 1963.


*Public Documents*

*Congressional Record,* 27 March, 1963.
*Congressional Record,* 27 May 1963.
*Congressional Record,* 10 September 1963.
*Congressional Record,* 21 October 1963.
U.S. Congress. *House Report,* 23 March 1962, of the Committee on Labor, Health, Education, Welfare Appropriations.
U.S. Congress, Committee on Interstate and Foreign Commerce. *House Resolutions, Bills to Provide Assistance in the Construction and Initial Operation of Community Mental Health Centers, and For Other Purposes.* Resolution No. 3688, No. 3689, No. 2567, 26, 27, and 28 March 1963.
U.S. Congress, Subcommittee of the Committee on Interstate and Foreign Commerce. *Report-Hearings on Mental Health* (Supplemental), 88th Congress, 1st Session, 10-11 July 1963.
U.S. Congress, U.S. Senate Subcommittee of the Committee on Appropriations—Department of Labor and HEW Appropriations for 1963, 10 April 1962, pp. 8-9.
U.S. Congress, Subcommittee on Health of the Committee on Labor and Public Welfare. *Senate Resolution, Bills to Provide Assistance in the Construction and Initial Operation of Community Mental Health Centers, and to Assist States in Combating Mental Retardation,* Resolution Nos. 755 and 756, 88th Congress, 1st Session, March 5, 6, and 7, 1963.
*Report-Hearings on Mental Health* (Supplemental) before a Subcommittee of the Committee on Interstate and Foreign Commerce. House of Representatives, 88th Congress, 1st Session on S. 1576, 10-11 July 1963.
U.S. Congress. Conference Report, *Mental Retardation Facilities and Community Mental Health Centers Construction Act of 1963.* Report No. 862, 88th Congress, 1st Session, October 21, 1963.
U.S. Congress. *Title II, Public Law 164 Community Mental Health Center Act of 1963.* 88th Congress, 1st Session, 1963.
*U.S. Congressional and Administrative News,* Vols. 1963-1967.

*Interviews*

In addition to all the interviews of chapters 1 and 2,
Mr. Robert Barclay, June 1972.
Mr. Wilbur Cohen, 14 May 1972.
Mr. James M. Menger, 7 June 1972.
Dr. George Tarjan, 29 July 1972.

# 4

# The Control of Regulations and Standards

When President Kennedy signed S. 1576 into Public Law 88-164, he remarked:

> Under this legislation, custodial mental institutions will be replaced by therapeutic centers. It should be possible, within a decade or two, to reduce the number of patients in mental institutions by 50 percent or more. The new law provides the tools with which we can accomplish this.[1]

The political process involved in fashioning "the tools" will be discussed in this chapter. Because the process involved a variety of powerful interest groups—an oligopoly of sorts—it had a high probability of achieving the staffing grants. In 1963 the NIMH leaders assumed the responsibility for the innovative and administrative aspects of a new categorical public policy. They functioned in an intricate web of tensions spun by historical circumstance and by coordinated, centralized design: congressional, presidential, judicial, group interest, intra-agency, interagency, intergovernmental, personal, societal, and even international. In the development, securing, and refinement of a major categorical program for the construction of community mental health centers, the controlling power of the mental health leadership becomes evident. These few—the mental health oligopoly—controlled the demand of the many buyers of a national health package wrapped, tied, and delivered in such a way as to change the total system.

As chapters 1 and 2 showed, the solutions to mental health problems demanded technical expertise in the bureaucracy and excellent political judgment in Congress.

Congress granted broad authority to the NIMH within very broadly construed limits outlined by the law. The unavoidable result of this trend was to enlarge gradually the political involvement of the mental health leadership in NIMH. This was accomplished by increasing reliance on professional experts within the bureaucracy as well as on outside experts as sources for new policy ideas, and by coercing the administrators to make decisions favorable to political interest groups such as the Lasker-Gorman axis. The broad administrative discretion of the NIMH director was due not merely to Felix's skill but also to an unavoidable fact of political life: The complex nature of the modern state necessitates that central elected officials delegate functions, responsibilities, and powers to administrators. The technological, empirical, and unpredictable dimensions of the environment of social conduct necessitate this delegation.

Theodore Lowi, noted political scientist, has commented:

> The complexity of modern life forces Congress into vagueness and generality in drafting its statutes. Admittedly, the political pressure of social unrest forces Congress and the President into premature formulations that make delegation of power inevitable. But to take these causes and effects as natural and good, and then to build the system around them, is to doom the system to remaining always locked into the original causes and effects.[2]

Lowi has developed in some depth the thesis that (1) the Congress irresponsibly delegates to the executive great authority in determining federal policies governing the expenditure of federal funds; (2) the federal agencies work with the affected, organized interest groups to develop and implement the regulations required, during which process the mass of the public is effectively cut out of the decision process; and (3) the development and overseeing of the regulations should be left to the courts.

The paradox exposed in the following pages is that in the case of Title II of Public Law 88-164, the Community Mental Health Centers Act, Congress and the president were not forced into vagueness or premature formulations but did, in fact, strengthen the Washington-based mental health monopoly through the regulations and standards, which in most aspects were consistent with the legislative intent of these elected officials. Although neither Congress nor the president was excluded from the formulation of administrative policy in the treatment of mental illness, they were not the key actors. Instead, the NIMH staff, with the cooperation of the National Advisory Mental Health Council, established the regulations. No one seems to have acted irresponsibly, despite the exclusion of the direct participation of the general public from the process.

**Public Law 88-164**

The statement of the law is less specific than the regulations and would seem to confirm Lowi's position. In fact, Congress and the president were aware of much of the content of the regulations and standards that the NIMH leadership, at Secretary Celebrezze's direction, would promulgate. Further, all were agreed that the law, with its regulations and standards, implemented their goal of phasing out the warehousing of patients in state mental hospitals. Indeed, the NIMH staff had been formulating the substantive content of the regulations and standards while they were designing the legislative package.

## Formulation of the Regulations

*Phase I: Within the Institute*

There were two types of professional orientation within NIMH in early 1963, with some degree of overlap: the supporters of the "medical" model and those of the "public health" model. The conflict was sometimes intense, but the NIMH leadership did not allow it to surface outside the institute.

Supporters of the "medical" or "sickness" model tended to advocate therapeutic strategies that emphasized reduction of conflict and enhancement of functioning by means of carefully established interpersonal relationships between provider (in most cases, a psychiatrist) and the patient.

The public health supporters allied themselves with the "social competence" supporters, who stressed ego-supportive approaches to help individuals develop their social competence in a rapidly moving technological world. The agents of such an approach were psychologists, teachers, nurses, special educators, police, judges, lawyers, clergy, physicians, and indigenous workers.

The conflict between the proponents of the public health model and the medical model supporters was resolved through compromise. A legislative program should be designed to reduce social disability resulting from mental illness, but at the same time, it should be acceptable to the private practitioners in psychiatry and medicine.

Data gathered in various community mental health facilities within and outside the United States guided the NIMH staff.[3] The staff and others traveled throughout the country, as well as in Europe, to study community mental health facilities. Dr. A. Querido from Holland and Maxwell Jones from Great Britain came to America and spoke of their experience with emergency care and therapeutic communities. The Milbank Foundation sent superintendents of state hospitals to Great Britain to observe the open mental hospitals. Staff of NIMH were not only aware of the community programs in Canada and Colorado; they also continued to run their own experimental comprehensive mental health program in Prince George's County, Maryland.[4]

From observation and experience, the staff put together a package of services: inpatient; outpatient; partial hospitalization and emergency services; and early diagnosis and treatment. Education and consultation to community agencies and to professional personnel were added as another essential service designed to satisfy those concerned with improving positive mental health and/or preventing mental illness.

The goal of this service package was continuity of care in the community. As a consequence, diagnostic services, rehabilitation, and aftercare for state hospital patients were relegated to the supplementary service category, as were training and research. Ewalt, Tarjan, and Gorman, members of the National Advisory Mental Health Council, agreed to this professional-political compromise.

Prior to the testimony of the administration before the Hill and Harris committees, the NIMH staff prepared a briefing book that emphasized the concept of continuity of care and all of the services.[5] This later appeared in the regulations and standards printed in the *Federal Register,* a government publication that lists new federal rules and regulations. Wilbur Cohen briefed President Kennedy from the NIMH-prepared briefing book.[6]

Jones testified before Roberts's subcommittee on the specific services envisioned and the notions that these services would be provided within geographical areas, the poor would be covered, and the care of the mentally ill would be brought into the mainstream of medicine.

The president and the authorizing and appropriation committees knew the substantive service outline of the centers legislation. In fact, the published hearings before Hill and Harris made this information available to the general public. What the Congress, the president, and the public did not know was that NIMH would define the concept of continuity of care in terms of essential services and specific program criteria.

*Interdepartmental Struggle*

After the president signed the bill into law, "an internal bureaucratic fight of the worst kind occurred" over the regulations, according to Atwell.[7] That the construction aspects of the bill had been modeled on the Hill-Burton formula served as the pretext for the Hill-Burton Agency of the Public Health Service to demand control of the program and to administer it as a subsection of one of the specialized health facilities. Under Title II, Section 204, of Public Law 88-164, funds were available for states to construct community mental health centers. However, allotment was qualified by strict adherence to the congressionally specified Hill-Burton pattern, which required a detailed state plan. The state plan had to include designation of state responsibility, accountability, minimum standards for the operation of the centers, and programs based on a statewide inventory of existing facilities and surveys of need.

The NIMH staff interpreted Section 203(1-2) of Public Law 88-164 as saying that no center could be constructed without the provision of the essential services. The Hill-Burton staff in the Bureau of Medical Services argued against this interpretation. It did not consider, nor was it aware, that the NIMH leadership had not intended—and would not allow—the centers program to become another "bricks-and-mortar" program.[8] Hill-Burton staff members saw only the construction aspects of the law. They objected to the NIMH's prescription for programmatic service elements, rather than physical construction standards only, as a condition for the construction of the centers.

A construction program would leave the administration of the program to the Bureau of Medical Services, but a construction program tied to specific, mandatory mental health services provided the justification for the NIMH to control the program. Although both agencies utilized their congressional contacts, the question of whether NIMH or Hill-Burton would administer the act was finally settled by the surgeon general and Wilbur Cohen. Although the final resolution occurred after his death, President Kennedy did not expect or want the Hill-Burton agency to administer the program. He wanted a service program, not another Hill-Burton construction program.[9]

The stakes in this battle were high:

1. The mental health leadership considered the centers legislation the first step in the development of a service system. To allow construction of centers only if the essential services were included would create the need for the staffng provisions that were unobtainable in 1963.

2. Felix and Yolles thought that loss of the centers program could jeopardize the mission and autonomy of the institute. Between 1962 and 1963 the NIMH leadership had developed a major service program which, for the first time in the history of the institute, promised to provide the funds that would make the NIMH a real triad of research, training, and service components—a triad authorized in the 1946 Mental Health Act. The fiscal magnitude of that balance would also help to ensure the organizational survival of the mental health institutional base.

**NIMH's History of Bureaucratic Struggle.** The NIMH leaders had survived in an environment of constant bureaucratic intrigue and reorganization battles.[10] The 1948 and 1954 reorganizations of the Public Health Service, of which NIMH was a component, had not changed the basic structure. Although Shannon, the director of the National Institutes of Health, wanted NIMH to be primarily a research institute, for fifteen years Felix continued to use his broad authorization from the 1946 act to assure that the institute's mission would be wider. His real challenge came in 1959, however, when a study group appointed by Surgeon General Burney recommended the transfer of NIMH clinical and service training programs to a new Bureau of Health Services and Health Resources. NIMH would lose nonresearch training programs, community services, and the Title V project grants to other PHS units. In addition, the institute's Biometry Branch, concerned with national measures of mental illness and the patient population of mental institutions, would also be transferred to the new bureau. The suggested changes would mean not only a cut of about 45 percent in the NIMH budget but the destruction of the organizational triad of the institute.

Felix reacted quickly and decisively on January 23, 1960. Speaking before the Senate Appropriations Committee, he said that he envisioned an expansion, not a contraction, of NIMH. Support of fundamental research alone was not enough. Only by continued NIMH support of the application of research results could advances be made in the fight against mental illness, Felix said. And NIMH was the staff office in this fight.

Although Shannon considered a transfer of NIMH community services inevitable, he stayed out of the battle between the surgeon general and Felix. He allowed Felix to wage his own campaign for continuity.

In that campaign, the surgeon general was no match for Felix. As director of NIMH in 1960, Felix carried star rank, equivalent to the navy's rear admiral, lower grade. He was assistant surgeon general. He was a member of major health organizations, an officer in most of them: American Medical Association, American Psychiatric Association, American Psychological Association, National Association for Mental Health, American Public Health Association, National Medical Corrections Association, and National League of Nursing Education. His strategy, first learned in the early attempts to reorganize the Public Health Service, was to alert these professional associations. They, in turn, raised enough of a hue and cry with Congress to trap the surgeon general. Felix also threatened to resign, which, because of his stature, would embarrass the surgeon general. (Felix used the same tactics on Celebrezze when the secretary hesitated to include sufficient funds for the initial operating costs of the centers.) Next, Felix personally contacted Hill and Fogarty. Both responded favorably.

On June 14, 1960, Hill made clear the intent of Congress to the surgeon general: "The committee is definitely opposed to any transfer of the clinical training programs of the NIMH to any proposed overall training division of the Public Health Service." [11] Felix had not only defeated the surgeon general's attempt to dismember the NIMH, but in 1961, the institute obtained an appropriation of $100,000,000, about 33 percent higher than in 1960. In 1961, President Kennedy appointed a new surgeon general, Dr. Luther Terry, a person respected in the Public Health Corps and acceptable to both his friend Felix and his uncle, Senator Hill.

The events of this reorganization battle were fresh in the minds of Felix and his staff when they designed the centers legislation and retained the initiative in drafting the regulations and standards. They were well aware that other reorganization battles would arise. During his testimony before Roberts on July 10, 1963, Felix advocated, but did not obtain, separate bureau status for NIMH in order to protect its institutional integrity. The hearings of the centers program and Cohen's and Jones's recollections clearly indicate that the congressmen in the authorizing committees and the top administration staff expected NIMH to administer the new legislation, but the NIMH leaders were, nevertheless, concerned about guaranteeing their control of the program in the short as well as the long run.

After the passage of the centers legislation, Felix was in the process of retiring from the institute and phasing all the programs into the hands of Dr. Stanley Yolles. Felix's power and prestige as director would be lost to the institute. Although Yolles was, perhaps, the key architect of the centers program, he did not have the same firm associations with congress and professional groups as did Felix. Yolles's ability to lead in the development of the institute would rest primarily not on its historically secure components—research and manpower—but on the expansion of the service component focused on the centers program. His strategy to ensure NIMH autonomy in mental health was to increase the fiscal magnitude of the service component until it eventually equaled that of research and manpower.

Consequently, in the battle with the Hill-Burton group, had Yolles, backed by Felix and aided by Brown and Atwell, lost the program, his later leadership position, as well as the agenda of the mental health leadership for a new service system, would have been jeopardized. Yolles wanted the additional program direction tied to the fiscal patronage that the centers program potentially offered.[12]


*Phase II—The Delineation of the Regulations and Standards*

Within a period of five months, six persons drafted the regulations and standards for Public Law 88-164, supported by the backup work of the NIMH central staff coordinated by executive officer George Van Staden.

The six were: Felix, Brown, Dr. Joseph Douglass, Dr. Lucy Ozarin, atwell, and Harry Cain. Felix wanted the service component reduced to a comprehensive statement. Brown and Atwell defined the comprehensiveness of the program by reducing what had become known as "the laundry list" of services to a reasonably comprehensive minimum. Despite Atwell's pessimism about the benefits for the mentally ill of educational and other preventive services, Brown, with Felix's approval, insisted on their inclusion.

## Design of Regulations Within the Intent of Congress

Section 203 of the act required the secretary, after consultation with the Federal Hospital Council and the National Advisory Mental Health Council, to prescribe "the kinds of community mental health services needed to provide adequate mental health services for persons residing in a state." [13]

NIMH defined the essential elements of comprehensive mental health services as

1. inpatient services,
2. outpatient services,
3. partial hospitalization services—at least day care service,
4. emergency services provided twenty-four hours per day and available within at least one of the first three services listed above, and
5. consultation and educational services available to community agencies and professional personnel.

No center program could be funded without these five services.[14] In addition, these strategists hoped to impel the states to evolve more comprehensive programs by requiring the state plan [15] to include the five services mentioned, as well as diagnostic services, vocational and educational programs, precare and aftercare services in the community (foster home placement, home visiting, and halfway houses), training, and research and evaluation.[16] All these services were consistent with the testimony prepared for and presented by the Secretary and Jones in March 1963.

"The Criteria of Program" (54.212) was intended to place the treatment of the mentally ill into the mainstream of medicine in a one-class system of care with guaranteed continuity of care—again consistent with the intent of the president and the Congress, as reported by the Senate-House conferees.

## Design of Regulations Beyond the Intent of Congress

*Psychiatric Control of the Program*

An oligopolistic move on the part of the psychiatric professions is found in Section 54.212(c)(3). There is no congressional or presidential documentation of intent that each center's program be under the supervision and control of a psychiatrist, as this section requires. Except for traditional professional status rankings, there was no reason why psychologists, physicians, and lay administrators with expertise in mental health could not have had administrative control of the program. The NIMH leaders, many of whom were psychiatrists, designed a regulation that reflected the interests of the American Psychiatric Association in order to encourage its members to support the new program.[17] In the early 1960s the medical profession still had enough power to control any health program.

### The No-Residency Requirement

Under "Criteria of Program" one of the regulations reads: "(4) That the service of the program will not be denied to any person residing within the area served solely on the ground that such person does not meet a requirement for a minimum period of residence in such area."[18] This regulation is extraordinary, because it appears to be the first no-residency requirement in a categorical federal-state health program, and predates the Supreme Court decision of *Shapiro* v. *Thompson* in which welfare residency requirements were found unconstitutional. Atwell was the author of the regulation.[19]

In 1963 the debate over the welfare residency requirements of states had already begun. Mindful of the statement in Public Law 88-164 to "provide needed services for persons unable to pay," Atwell decided to formulate this regulation in a federal-state program. The regulation was consistent with the Equal Protection Clause of the Fourteenth Amendment. This fact can be seen only in retrospect, however, because not until 1966, in *Katzenback* v. *Morgan,* did the Court Rule: "Congress is without power to enlist state cooperation in a joint Federal-state program by legislation which authorizes the states to violate the Equal Protection Clause."[20] The argument could also be made that, without this regulation, states might have denied due process by unduly burdening the right of interstate travel of the mentally ill. Because no objection is recorded to this regulation, this was perhaps the implicit reasoning of the legal counsels to the Interstate and Foreign Commerce Committee and of the Legal Counsel Office of HEW. (It is also quite possible that the staff in the committee and HEW were preoccupied with other legislative matters. At the same time, the secretary's staff was involved in developing the Mental Health Interstate Compact, a reciprocal arrangement between states to cover the care of those mentally ill traveling across their borders. The staff was aware of Judge Bazelon's efforts to remove the residency requirement of the district during the same period.)

Nor was there any objection to the publication of the no-residency regulation in the *Federal Register*. A bureaucrat had formulated a law. Lack of an adversary procedure or political omission resulted in the implementation of that law. Atwell's action indicated positive, responsible foresight. It also illustrates that the regulations and standards of domestic programs can be a powerful political tool. As such, they may increasingly require clearer notification than by mere publication in the *Federal Register,* a source well known to interest groups but unknown to the general public.

### The Definition of Community

Public law 88-164, Section 203, assigned to the NIMH staff the problem of defining the limits of "community." Cain, under Atwell's supervision and with Felix's approval and direction, took on the task. He reviewed the social science literature and contacted several prominent social scientists; neither source agreed on the meaning of the term *community.* "We came down to simply 'numbers of people' because the other approaches—political, geographic, ethic, or socio-economic boundaries—did not work. 'Quantities of population' was the last resort." [21] Felix had stated in his congressional testimony before Hill and Harris that each center would serve approximately 100,000 persons. He arrived at this figure on the spur of the moment, by simply dividing the two thousand centers discussed in the president's task force into a population of 200,-000,000.

Consequently, Cain, Atwell, Brown, and Felix agreed to use that figure as a point of departure, refine the figure, and thus define the parameters of the community in terms of numbers of persons in geographical areas on the basis of economic, clinical, and political criteria. These criteria narrowed the arbitrariness of their definition. From an economic-clinical standpoint, if a community was defined as less than 50,000 persons, the unit costs would be prohibitive; if it was defined as above 200,000 persons, the centers would become mob scenes, and clinicians would be overwhelmed with patients. The political sense of these men dictated that, should they set the minimum figure at 50,000, certain sections of the country would attempt to construct centers "on every corner" and would shortly bankrupt the program. Discussion on the maximum figure ranged from 150,000 persons to 250,000 persons, with little political weight given these figures. In the end, they settled on the range 75,000 to 200,000 persons within given geographical areas.

Regulation 54.203(b)(2) requires:

The state plan shall provide that every community mental health facility shall:
(i) Serve a population of not less than 75,000 and not more than 200,000 persons, except that the Surgeon General may, in particular cases, permit modifications of this population range if he finds that

such modifications will not impair the effectiveness of the services to be provided;

(ii) Be so located as to be near and readily accessible to the community and population to be served, taking into account both political and geographical boundaries.[22]

The intent of Congress was to provide a mental health service program to the general public. The NIMH staff developed a program, under the control of psychiatrists, that provided services within specific geographical boundaries not to include more than 200,000 persons (later to be called "catchment areas" in NIMH literature, but not in the act or its regulations). A few of the staff thought that designing Section 203(b)(2) as they did could occasion the development of two thousand monopolistic mental health service centers, two thousand mental health centers responsible to the public as a new type of public utility. This dream was unlikely to be fulfilled, because Congress did not intend that the two thousand be monopolistic, and the dream ignored the cultural reality that the American consumer did not view his health system as a public utility. Reasoned public debate or juridical review, as Lowi recommends, might not have changed the wording of this regulation, because the wording did not violate the intent of Congress. Where such review would appear appropriate, however, is in the implementation of the regulations in order to determine whose intent is fulfilled—the Congress or the professional elite in the bureaucracy.

*The Budgetary and Staffing Pattern*

Section 54.212(d) required that applications for construction funds include a description of the proposed sources of operating income for all service elements included in the program, plus the proposed staffing pattern by major professional categories for all elements.[23] This requirement would highlight the need for initial staffing grants. When most potential applicants realized the cost reality of any viable operating program budget —one that would cover needed services and professionals—it was likely that the middle-income groups would demand congressional action to support staffing. Acceptance of the service program as a necessary condition for approval of the construction grants underscored the need for additional funding to assist local communities.

## Role of the National Advisory Mental Health Council

Dr. Joseph Douglass presented the NIMH staff work on the regulations and standards to members of the Advisory Council: Dr. John J. Blasko

(VA), Dr. Ralph L. Christy (USN), Dr. Jack R. Ewalt, Mr. Armand Gilinsky, Dr. Louis S. Goodman, Mr. Mike Gorman, Dr. George C. Ham, Mrs. Geri Joseph, Dr. Charles R. Strother, Dr. George Tarjan, Senator Robert D. Williams, Dr. Robin M. Williams, Jr., Dr. Cecil L. Wittson, and Dr. Dale Wolfle. The council membership was weighted toward the psychiatric interest groups. Ewalt, Gorman, and Tarjan played major roles in gaining approval of most of the presentation.

The regulations adequately reflected the professional positions of the psychiatrists and satisfied the interest of the American Psychiatric Association. Section 54.212(2) requires: "That a qualified psychiatrist will be responsible for the clinical program and the medical responsibility for every patient will be vested in a physician." [24] Quick initiation of the program by NIMH administrators would meet Gorman's need for dramatic action. During the meetings on March 19-21, 1964, "the National Advisory Mental Health Council unanimously and enthusiastically recommended approval of the proposed regulations with certain modifications." [25] Shortly thereafter, Yolles, Van Staden, Douglass, and Atwell went to Amsterdam to observe how Querido's program operated.

When NIMH submitted the regulations to the Office of the General Counsel, DHEW, Wilbur Cohen approved them with the realization that Section 54.212 would set the stage for later authorization of the staffing grants, probably in a relatively short time. [26]

On May 6, 1964, the regulations were published in the *Federal Register* and became effective on the date of publication. Normally, there is a period of thirty days before the regulations published in the *Federal Register* become effective. This period, bypassed in this case, gives interested citizens the opportunity to present objections and to recommend modifications to the regulations, prior to their enforcement.

The absence of a waiting period precluded any opportunity to object. Consequently, it is not surprising that there is no record of opposition to the regulations in the files of the general counsel, DHEW, of NIMH's legal section, or in the records of the Justice Department. As far as can be determined through interviews with knowledgeable parties, no comments about the regulations from citizens found their way to the congressional and staff members of the House Committee on Interstate and Foreign Commerce, which would have served as the congressional channel to HEW in this matter.

It is unlikely that any strong opposition would have occurred from within the mental health oligopoly. By means of the hospital improvement program and the hospital staff development program, the NIMH leadership had already defused the opposition of the state mental hospital administrators. Also, by March 1962, thirteen states had passed enabling, but not mandatory, community mental health service acts. Many of these acts provided reimbursement for operating costs, including salaries of professional personnel for the five essential services listed in the regulation of Public Law 88-164, but they excluded reimbursement for construction of buildings and capital improvements.[27] Public Law 88-164 gave these thirteen states needed financial assistance for construction. Any division of opinion on the regulations could await later developments on the staffing regulations or be resolved by bargaining within the oligopoly.


## The Oligopolistic Process

Throughout the late fifties and early sixties, the mental health leadership had acted as an oligopoly. Government officials and interest group members had defined the mental health problem: the warehousing of the mentally ill. A public altered by the mental health leaders demanded resolution of the problem. The technical nature of that problem demanded that the professional expertise within the oligopoly present an alternative to state mental hospitals; such development was outside the ability of the average citizen. The process by which community mental health centers became the legal alternative points out the hierarchical nature of the mental health oligopoly.

The NIMH leaders specified the content of the law. Throughout 1964 and 1965, they and their allies—Ewalt, Cohen, Gorman, Barton, to name a few—bargained over the regulations and standards. All involved checked the NIMH staff control to a degree, although none doubted that NIMH Director Felix would control the direction of the program.

By the time the regulations and standards were formulated, NIMH had pre-empted that control. The mental health groups were willing to submerge their differences, as they had during the congressional battle over the centers program, in order to obtain the desired alternative to the warehousing of patients.

Political theorist Lowi argues that when interest groups are so wedded to bureaucracies that the very thought processes of the bureaucrats are influenced in favor of those groups, the electorate is bypassed in policy formation. The discretionary power of the governmental agency is broader than intended by Congress. This theoretical position isn't borne out by the political facts touching the 1963 mental health movement. The character of public control in the formulation of Public Law 88-164 was both voluntary and involuntary: NIMH represented the interest groups supporting mental health, but it also was sensitive to the intent of Congress in formulating regulations and standards for implementing the community mental health center legislation.

There were legal check-off points; the regulations had to pass through several hands, any one of which could have sent them back for modification: the secretary of HEW and the Justice Department, both responsible to the will of Congress, had to approve them. They had to appear in the *Federal Register,* where, technically, interested citizens have access to proposed regulations and standards and, in most cases, are able to challenge them. (The *Register,* however, is relatively unknown to the general public because it is circulated on a subscription basis.)

The remarkable aspects of the process of law making in 1963-64, though indeed historically limited, do not indicate a bastardization of the constitutional process but rather an accommodation of Congress to technocratic agencies. Knowledgeable congressional leaders did authorize the centers program with the specific intent to provide local services to the mentally ill. At the same time, they allowed the NIMH administrators to satisfy their own moral convictions through regulations to implement Public Law 88-164. The special biases, backgrounds, and interests of the NIMH cadre, plus their own moral convictions, would guide the eventual compromises.

As long as the compromises did not violate the intent of the Congress, congressional intervention was unnecessary. Automatic reference back to the authority of Congress about each specific would have only delayed the process and would have indicated a lack of administrative ability on the part of NIMH leaders. The flexibility allowed by Congress was a necessary prerequisite for the positive public policy determination on the requirements that the centers program would be primarily a service program in the mainstream of medicine and not a construction program.

As Lowi points out, however, rule making has involuntary aspects, and the tendency of oligopoly is to reduce competition. Certainly, the NIMH leaders' definition of community and their designation of psychiatric control of the centers highlight these dangers.

Relative to the NIMH leadership, two questions arose then: (1) Did the mental health oligopoly foreclose on disagreement from any sector? (2) Did it accommodate or submit to pressure groups, thereby sacrificing its initial ideals and new modalities? Lowi writes:

When a program is set up in a specialized agency, the number of organized interest groups surrounding it tends to be reduced precisely to those groups and factions to whom the specialization is most salient. That in turn tends to reduce the situation from one of potential competition to potential oligopoly. That is to say, one can observe numerous groups in some kind of competition for agency favors. But competition tends to last only until each group learns the goals of the few other groups. Each adjusts to the others. Real confrontation leads to the net loss for all rather than gain for any. Rather than countervailing power, there will more than likely be accommodating power.[28]

The mental health oligopoly highlighted the problem of warehousing of the mentally ill; it prescribed community programs as its solution, but not as a cure of all mental illness. The centers program expanded the NIMH leaders' purchasing power through the awarding of grants and a new constituency: mental health centers' directors, trustees, staff, and those patients treated in local communities.

Concomitantly, the service program also offered a potential set of problems. The center alternative and its adaptation in local communities would lead to other alternatives, while new treatment modalities developed (often through the support of NIMH research funds) and while major social shifts (such as the emphasis on citizen participation) occurred in the sixties. New groups and influential unorganized citizens would confront the oligopoly keyed on the NIMH and demand that the NIMH promote their causes and include them in the oligopoly; these were unintended consequences. Questions arise then. Should the oligopoly expand, subsuming new interests and modalities under its ideals? Particularly, should the oligopoly continue, since without its expertise in mental health programs, the mentally ill would lack an effective political voice in Washington and in the state capitals where programs are funded?

According to Lowi:

Programs of this sort tend to cut out all that part of the mass that is not specifically organized around values strongly salient to the goals of the program. They shut out the public, first, at the most creative phase of the policy making—the phase where the problem is defined.[29]

There was only foreclosure on the public in the NIMH's definitive planning of the regulations, primarily because the general public is uninformed of the significance of the *Federal Register* and has no incentive to subscribe to it, and the *Register* itself may be an inadequate legal tool. The fact that the public was not shut out at the phase of definition of the problem of warehousing suggests the possibility that an oligopoly—at least in the mental health sector—can include the public in a phase of policy making. An expanded professional-citizen oligopoly, hierarchically centered on a governmental mental health or health agency responsible to the Congress, to the president, and to the courts, would obviate Lowi's objection to lack of public involvement. The critical factors for the mental health of the nation are not simply the structure and process characteristics. Just as important are the commitment of mental health professionals, of concerned citizens, and of elected officials, along with their ability to compromise in an attempt to reach realistic humane goals. That pattern of characteristics explains why the legislation for the total center program became a reality in 1965. And that pattern, as historically defined, suggests how major social policy change can occur in this decade. In essence, it is the pattern of centralized decision making in a technological and constitutional society. The oligopoly brings policy to fruition. Outside of a technocratic-political oligopoly, professional expertise is neither sustained nor funded to develop viable alternative policies or to ensure their implementation. Basic premises for such a conclusion, of course, are responsibility within the oligopoly itself and its frequent accountability on substantive policies to the president and to the Congress. One of the tasks of both the president and the Congress is to provide effective mechanisms to the citizen for his involvement in the creative phase of policy making. The *Federal Register* may not be sufficient.

The court-dominated solution that Lowi offers, however, is too slow and technologically inappropriate to deal with the complex evolution of a national mental health program. An oligopolistic approach, bounded by constitutional restraints and under the control of responsible administrators, but checked by an informed public, offers the likelihood of a timely mental health program open to later evolutionary modifications. The events of 1963 to 1965 support this view.

The untimely death of President John Kennedy deprived the mental health oligopoly of its proudest champion in the midst of unfinished business. There was the matter of the unobtained staffing grants. What would be the reaction of Lyndon Johnson, now president, a man of individualistic nature, of possible new priorities, and of considerable congressional influence? Predictably, there would be new alignments and interest blocks ahead.

Could the mental health leadership take them in stride on its way to successful completion of its program?

# Notes

1. "JFK's Remarks as He Signed Into Law Mental Health-Retardation Centers Bill (S. 1576)," White House, 31 October 1963.

2. Theodore J. Lowi, *The End of Liberalism* (New York: W. W. Norton and Company, Inc., 1969), p. 155.

3. "Construction of Community Mental Health Facilities: Planning, Financing and Legal Mechanisms," May 1962, NIMH Files.

4. Detailed Proposal from NIMH Files, dated 3 August 1962. William G. Hollister, M.D., made NIMH staff aware of the comprehensive community psychiatric program at Montifiore Hospital, New York.

5. *Briefing Book for Secretary on Community Mental Health Centers of 1963,* NIMH Files.

6. Interview with Cohen, 14 June 1972.

7. Interview with Atwell, 26 January 1972.

8. Interview with Cain, 5 February 1972.

9. Interview with Feldman, 19 August 1972.

10. Edith Carper, "The Reorganization of the Public Health Service," The Inter-University Care Program (New York, November 1961). Draft, III-14.

11. Quoted by Carper, from Appropriation Hearings, 14 June 1960, Ibid., VII-12.

12. Interview with Dr. Stanley Yolles, 23 March 1972.

13. Public Law 88-164, 88th Congress, S. 1576, October 31, 1963, Section 203.

14. Section 54.212, Community Mental Health Centers Act of 1963, Title II, Public Law 88-164, Regulations, *Federal Register,* 6 May 1964, p. 5955.

15. The Hill-Burton formula required a state plan.

16. Section 54.203, *Federal Register,* p. 5952.

17. Interview with Cain, 5 February 1972.

18. Section 54.212, *Federal Register,* p. 5955.

19. Interview with Robert Atwell, 16 August 1972.

20. *Katzenback v. Morgan,* 383 vs 641, 651, n. 10 16L Ed 2d 828, 836 86S Ct, 1717, 1966.

21. Interview with Dr. Harry Cain II, 27 December 1971, and Dr. Robert H. Felix, 17-18 February 1972.

22. Section 54-203, *Federal Register,* p. 5952.

23. Section 54-212, *Federal Register,* p. 5955.

24. Ibid.

25. Minutes of the National Advisory Mental Health Council, 19-21 March 1964, p. 30.

26. Interview with Wilbur Cohen, 14 June 1972.
27. Lucy D. Ozarin, M.D., "Recent Community Mental Health Legislation—A Brief Review," A.J.P.H. 52, no. 3 (March 1962).
28. Lowi, p. 295.
29. Ibid., p. 86.

## Bibliography

*Books*

Cleveland, Harlem and Harold D. Lasswell, eds. *Ethics and Bigness.* New
York: Harper and Brothers, 1962.
Lowi, Theodore J. *The End of Liberalism.* New York: W. W. Norton and
Company, Inc., 1969.

*Articles and Memoranda*

Carper, Edith. "The Reorganization of the Public Health Service." The
Inter-University Care Program. New York, November 1961. Draft,
III-14.
Cain, Harry P., II, and Lucy D. Ozarin. "Hospitals and the Community
Mental Health Centers Program." *Hospitals J.A.H.A.* 38, no. 24 (De-
cember 16, 1964).
Ozarin, Lucy D. "Recent Communtiy Mental Health Legislation—A Brief
Review." *A.J.P.H.* 52, no. 3 (March 1962).
"Construction of Community Mental Health Facilities: Planning, Financ-
ing, and Legal Mechanisms," May 1962, NIMH Files.
Detailed Proposal from NIMH Files, 3 August 1962. William G. Hollister,
M.D., made NIMH staff aware of the comprehensive community psychi-
atric program at Montifiore Hospital, New York.
*Briefing Book for Secretary on Community Mental Health Centers of 1963,*
NIMH Files.
Minutes of the National Advisory Mental Health Council, 19-21 March
1964.

*Public Documents*

*Community Mental Health Centers Act of 1963,* Title II, Public Law
88-164. Regulations, *Federal Register,* 6 May 1964.

*Katzenbach* v. *Morgan,* 384 vs. 641, 651, n. 10 16L Ed 2d 828, 836, 86 S Ct., 1717, 1966.

*Interviews*

All previous interviews plus
Dr. Harry P. Cain, II, 27 December 1971 and 5 February 1973.

# 5

## The Passage of the Staffing Grants

By the first half of 1964, the mental health leadership and their allies had obtained authorization for the service-oriented construction of mental health centers—half of their goal. In the latter half of 1964 and throughout 1965, the NIMH-coordinated political actors tailored their strategies to coincide with the skillful parliamentary approach of President Lyndon B. Johnson. As a consequence, they achieved their total policy objective: a national community mental health program.

After July 1964, it became apparent that the careful skewing of the regulations of Public Law 88-164 to assure the delivery of services could not alone elicit continued political support. Field trips and other activities had convinced the NIMH central staff that very few states would submit state plans in the first year. It had become clear during the Institute-sponsored Appalachia Conference that the bricks-and-mortar nature of the program gave it relatively low priority in the "have-not" states, which desperately needed the services themselves before new buildings. Furthermore, the appropriated $35,000,000 was a negligible sum of money in the larger states and was wholly inadequate to achieve the objectives of the president's program.

President Johnson intended to clean up the essential unfinished domestic business begun by John F. Kennedy. He had informed HEW of his intention to take care of the most crucial issues.

In July 1964, four months before the general election, Robert Atwell assessed the political consequences for the mental health program of having Johnson as president. Atwell had left the Bureau of the Budget, joined the institute, and had become the first deputy to Dr. Bertram S. Brown, who had administrative responsibility for the centers program. In a concise, six-page position paper, Atwell recommended that the NIMH and other interested individuals and organizations should take action *immediately* toward the goal of obtaining additional legislative authority to support the operation of community mental health programs.[1]

Atwell argued that the time for a new initiative for mental health staffing was the fall of 1964, because the next January would see a newly elected president and a new Congress. He predicted that President Johnson would be elected by a substantial majority in November and that the new Congress would be politically more liberal. He also noted that there were other changes in the "congressional complexion," such as weakened ties between Oren Harris, chairman of the House Committee on Interstate and Foreign Commerce, and the American Medical Association.

Atwell went on to speculate that President Johnson would be more aggressive in seeking passage of his legislative programs than was President Kennedy—and that Johnson was eager to put his own stamp on those programs. He added another prediction: "The projected decline in defense expenditures together with the probable increase in tax revenues because of economic growth (at least on a cyclical basis) point to some opportunities for increases in social welfare program support." [2]

Atwell mentioned that Assistant Secretary Wilbur Cohen had raised the subject of mental health staffing subsidies as an item for consideration by Johnson's Task Force on Health Services. Prior to outlining steps to implement the recommendation, Atwell argued that immediate legislative initiative would result in progress in the centers program and counteract efforts to dismember NIMH during the immediate post-Felix period.

He suggested that the implementation of the president's legislative program follow some of the basic lines of the strategy of 1962-63:

1. inclusion of the proposal by the Task Force on Health Services,
2. inclusion of the proposal in the Democratic party platform (which did not occur),
3. presentation of the proposal to key White House officials and to the Bureau of the Budget,
4. utilization of mental retardation forces,
5. support of key congressional leaders,
6. mobilization of key professional agencies and individuals, and
7. supporting staff work.

He identified the key persons to be contacted. Just as the early planning and proposals in the field of child health and mental retardation had been formulated during the campaign and preinaugural period of the Kennedy administration, Atwell wanted the staffing proposal developed in the Johnson campaign. In his position paper, a memorandum to Yolles's deputy, Dr. Philip Sirotkin, Atwell argued: "We have everything to gain and nothing to lose through immediate action." [3] Sirotkin agreed.[4]

Sirotkin discussed the strategy with Yolles, who at first resisted. Gorman had persuaded Yolles that he should not request further substantive legislation until *concrete* programs" had been achieved—until centers had been constructed. In Gorman's view, NIMH had yet to "tangibilitate" the centers—"get the buildings up." Gorman held to the viewpoint that the defeat on the staffing provisions was too recent.[5] Yolles came around to the Atwell-Sirotkin position, however, and ran a bureaucratic end run around the surgeon general.[6] He reached an understanding with Cohen that, when the time was ripe, the administration would introduce the staffing legislation.[7] On November 1, 1964, Johnson stated his policy: "We must step up the fight on mental health and mental retardation. I intend to ask for increased funds for research centers, for special teacher training, and for helping coordinated state and local programs."[8] Yolles directed the NIMH staff to develop the legislative package.

Their original package proposed wider discretionary power for NIMH than that passed by the Senate in S. 1576, the rejected original staffing bill. The suggested legislation was not limited to initial staffing or to the support of projects for which the federal government provided construction assistance under the Hill-Burton formula. For the approval of programs in local communities, Yolles, Sirotkin, and Atwell agreed to the concept of by-passing the states. Atwell wanted priority eventually given to programs for the poor. Sirotkin favored this approach, while Yolles wanted a universal approach, covering any income group. The supporting documents included a state-by-state analysis of the status of the centers program and of the inability within existing PHS authority to meet the objectives of the president's program.

The staff developed projections on increased insurance coverage in order to answer the question of how the local communities would be able to finance fully the centers program once the federal funds had decreased. That the United Auto Workers' contract and the Federal Employees Health Benefits program included mental illness insurance programs and that the proposed Medicare program might cover mental health benefits for senior citizens suggested that other industry, labor, professional, and insurance groups would expand their mental health benefits. Yet, it was only an outside chance that insurance coverage would grow fast enough to cover the operating costs of the centers. The concept of multiple sources of funding—initial federal funds, state, local, and insurance monies—was an acceptable political strategem. Yolles, Sirotkin, Atwell, and other NIMH staff anticipated a further progression to greater federal investment on the local level. "We weren't kidding ourselves about this. At the end of eight years, we'd renew," Sirotkin recalled recently.[9] Yolles also wanted the establishment of two thousand centers.

Yolles and his staff did not voice that view publicly, even to the American Psychiatric Association, because the psychiatric profession was divided on whether the federal government should assume a permanent role. Further, they had not discussed it with Cohen. Some APA members, such as Jack Ewalt, however, were aware that adequate mental health insurance coverage might take at least a decade to evolve.[10] Cohen's approach was to use decreasing funding of a categorical program—the gradual decrease of the proportion contributed by the federal government. If continued federal funding was needed in the future, he was likely to support an extension of federal assistance, "I only accepted the declining proportion because it was the only way to get Secretary Celebrezze's approval without extensive internal discussion and delay." [11] Cohen calculated that a decreasing staffing grant approach would give . . "us more flexibility on how much to fund the program and how it would grow" [12] Both the NIMH strategists and Cohen doubted that Fogarty or Hill feared indefinite federal financing.

By November, Gorman's discussions with Yolles, coupled with Johnson's electoral triumph, convinced Gorman to coordinate his efforts with other lobbyists and the NIMH. He felt compelled to assume a major role in the push for the financing of initial operations of community mental health centers. Johnson had gathered in the largest plurality in the history of the country, nearly 16 million voters, or 61.1 percent of the electorate. He had swept the Democratic Eighty-ninth Congress in on his coattails.

Before the expected attrition of public support set in, Johnson proposed to use his victory first for his medical and education bills. Medicare offered the opportunity to distract the American Medical Association from other medical bills, such as the staffing grant proposal.

President Johnson's early approach to Congress coincided with the mental health coalition's strategy. He would propose only the legislation that had been garnering public support for so long that most congressmen would vote for it or risk losing the next election. Johnson's strategy also called for sending bills to Congress when the committee slates were clear enough to permit the legislation to move swiftly through the legislative process, a tactic that foreclosed a build-up of opposition and also took advantage of the enthusiasm of supporters when it was ripest.

On December 10, 1964, the mental health leadership met to discuss the proposed legislation. The group was composed of Michael Amrine (American Psychological Association), Dr. Walter E. Barton (American Psychiatric Association), Mike Gorman, Robert L. Robinson (American Psychiatric Association), Philip E. Ryan and Harry Milt (National Association for Mental Health, Inc.), Harry Schnibbe (National Association of State Mental Health Program Directors), Dr. Stanley Yolles, and Sirotkin. These members, along with Bert Seidman (AFL-CIO), would coordinate their lobbying activities. Felix, Ewalt, Braceland, and other members of the Group for the Advancement of Psychiatry would be supportive but no longer controlling. The presence of these groups was important, because Yolles, Sirotkin, and Atwell were less deferential to the states than were the lobbyists and the institute, led by Felix. The legislation proposed by Yolles and his staff would not leave the states empty-handed in terms of money, but it would minimize their control.

At the annual meeting of the States and Territorial Mental Health

Authorities with the surgeon general (January 5, 6, and 7), the discussion centered not on the issue of whether there should be staffing grants but on their length. The state mental health program directors, especially those from states with community mental health legislation, viewed the grants as advantageous and supplemental to their states' efforts. County directors, especially in California, desired this new source of financing. Yolles and Sirotkin also emphasized to the state directors the increase in the Hospital Improvement Program (HIP), and Hospital Improvement of Staffing Program (HIS) budgets.

On January 13, 1965, V. Terrel Davis, M.D., president of the National Association of State Mental Health Program Directors, at the direction of the Board of Directors conveyed to Yolles their recommendations:

(1) There should be federal financial support for operational expenses of community mental health center programs and for the establishment of new segments of mental health programs leading to comprehensive community mental health services which may or may not involve new construction.

(2) High initial support with rapid reduction of federal financial support is much less valuable than a lower level of support on a continuing basis.

(3) Support for non-patient care costs (such as administration, education, and consultation) particularly merit federal support.

(4) The Association supports the Long-Carlson Amendment to the Social Securtiy Act and is in favor of the removal of the exclusions of payment of services for the mentally ill in the King-Anderson and other comprehensive health legislation.[13]

State directors voiced opposition in at least three instances: Lowry of California objected to NIMH by-passing the state in the approval of the staffing grants.[14] Dr. David Vail of Minnesota objected to the whole center concept as ill conceived.[15] Dr. William Schumacher thought the concept laudable but not necessarily appropriate for Maine.[16] But their organization kept the opposition "in house" and presented a stance of unanimity favorable to the staffing grants.

Gorman and Ryan used their citizen organizations to mount an effective, grass-roots letter-writing campaign. Mrs. Winthrop Rockefeller, president of the National Association for Mental Health, mobilized forces in Arkansas close to Representative Oren Harris. Dr. Harold Visotsky, state mental health director of Illinois, had been able to reach Representative Springer (Ill.).

Dr. Walter Barton, of the American Psychiatric Association, negotiated with the leadership of the American Medical Association for their muted, rather than all-out, opposition to the staffing grants. APA offered its support as a medical specialty to the AMA at a time when the complexion of AMA organizational membership was shifting from general practitioners to specialists.[17]

Prior to the inauguration, the strategy had paid off. The administration and the key congressional leaders would sponsor a staffing bill. Wilbur Cohen had briefed Johnson on every aspect of the legislation. Gorman had met with the congressional leaders.

On January 7, 1965, President Johnson delivered his health message to Congress, in which there was a section on "Improved Community Mental Health Services":

> Few communities have the funds to support adequate programs, particularly during the first years.
> Communities with the greatest needs are hesitant to build centers without being able to identify the source of operating funds.
> Most of the people in need are children, the aged, or patients with low income.
> I, therefore, recommend legislation to authorize a five-year program of grants for the initial cost personnel to man community mental health centers which offer comprehensive services.[18]

The theme about the children, the aged, the poor was consistent with Kennedy's special message. The service program was of the mental health coalition's design. Choosing the right moment for proposing it was Johnson's.

On January 19, 1965, Representative Oren Harris introduced H.R. 2985, "to authorize assistance in meeting the initial cost of professional and technical personnel for comprehensive community mental health centers." Senator Lister Hill introduced the same bill in the Senate as S. 513. James A. Menger, a member of Harris's committee staff, and Robert Barclay, one of Hill's staff members, were critical expediters of the bills and links to Yolles and Sirotkin.[19] Both Menger and Barclay felt that at that point Johnson could obtain anything he wanted from the Eighty-ninth Congress.[20]

### The Psychiatric Conference

In December 1964, Sirotkin broached the tactic of a banquet to mobilize political support. On February 20, 1965, the American Psychiatric Association gathered five hundred experts from various fields to discuss plans for the new community mental health centers. The conference was represented by over 30,000 citizens in communities throughout the nation who had become involved in the planning process after the 1963 congressional appropriation of funds. The participants represented the state mental health authorities, the district branches, state NAMH chapters, and the state medical societies. National invitees included the presidents of both APAs, the American Medical Association, the secretary of health, education, and welfare, the vice-president of the National Council of Churches, the president of the American Nurses Association, the governor of Illinois, and Walter Reuther—a formidable array of dignitaries.

Mrs. Rockefeller set the tone of the conference: "A network of shiny new buildings without initial provision for operating and maintaining their buildings is no answer to better care for the mentally ill." [21] Cohen noted that President Johnson desired the staffing funds and that Congress had decided against including staff money in the 1963 act largely because of AMA opposition. Gorman and Felix issued the call for the acceleration of mental health training programs to provide the needed personnel for community mental health programs. Dr. Donovan F. Ward, AMA president, again defended the organization's stand on the staffing issue, but hedged:

> The AMA is firmly committed to the proposition that the local community is most responsive to the health needs of its citizens and that it should assume the basic responsibility for their needs. The next level is that of state government and if its resources prove inadequate then there is the Federal Government. [22]

At the closing banquet, Harris, Fogarty, and Hill were seated at the head table. Harris challenged the audience: "I hope we can get this bill passed but I want you to know that it is highly controversial and you'd better get busy and muster all the support you can find for it in every nook and cranny of this land." [23]

Senator Hill rose to credit the 1963 defeat of the staffing provisions to the vigorous opposition of the AMA. But, "I say to you, our defeat was only a temporary one. This time we will not be denied." [24] The mental health leadership and their congressional allies had effectively mobilized their constituencies. The participants at the conference passed a resolution, by acclamation, that the conference:

(1) Seconds President Johnson's recommendations to the Congress that Federal assistance be provided for the staffing of community mental health centers;

(2) Endorses Senate Bill S. 513 and H.R. 2985 to implement the President's recommendation; and

(3) Urges that a coordinated and sustained effort be initiated by the American Psychiatric Association, aided by the National Association for Mental Health, and similarly dedicated groups and individuals to develop a national consensus of support so as to make possible the achievement of our common national goal of adequate community mental health services for all citizens.[25]

## Congressional Action

*Hearings Before the House Committee on Interstate and Foreign Commerce*

On March 2, 3, 4, and 5, 1965, Oren Harris conducted hearings on H.R. 2985 before the full committee. The witnesses for the administration were ready, and Gorman, assisted by the other lobbyists, had groomed a battery of articulate leaders from the states and local communities. In this instance, Gorman's skill favorably impressed members and staff of the committee. His assistance made their legislative task easier.

After Secretary Celebrezze testified on the overall legislative package, he delegated Yolles to handle the testimony on the staffing provisions. Yolles addressed himself to the issues of the need for staffing, its temporary quality, its form, and NIMH's practical concern about state mental hospitals. His testimony reveals the following:

1. No center facilities were under construction in March of 1965 because the money became available in November 1964 and the state plans, mandatory by law, had not come in as yet. No application could be approved until the state plan was approved. Certain communities would not submit plans until they were assured of operating costs.

2. Representative Springer did not want to see the administration come back for an extension. Yolles stated that this event was unlikely, because the communities were prepared to deal with the problem of phasing out the federal funds.

3. On the form of the staffing provisions, Yoles testified:

It is proposed that the staffing grants not be on a formula basis, but rather, be on a project-grant basis so that their funds can be administered flexibly, at least in the beginning of the program, and so that those communities that are ready to move forward and extend their services, and also those comunities that are in most need can be assisted.[26]

The project grant basis gave the administrative authority to the federal administrators.

4. Yolles emphasized the HIP and HIS programs to demonstrate NIMH's concern with the patients then in the state mental hospitals. He mentioned that the increasing size of the mental health manpower pool, fed by NIMH funds, would prevent the shift of scarce manpower in state mental hospitals to community programs.[27]

When Yolles had finished, Gorman's drum roll of witnesses started.

Isadore Tuerk, M.D., commissioner of Maryland's Department of Mental Hygiene, testified for the National Association of State Mental Health Program Directors and provided specific data on the clinical appropriateness and cost savings of the community mental health center. He added a remark about the state role:

> It is our hope that Federal assistance staffing community mental health centers will stimulate the eventual operation of most centers not by the states, but by local, private, non-profit organizations. The local organizations today cannot afford to initiate and staff a mental health center. The state is—we hope—a temporary intermediary.[28]

He emphasized the need to attract graduates of professional training programs into the community mental health centers by providing decent, competitive salary levels initially provided by the federal government. "Money which communities can gradually supplant once their centers have been "catapulated" into existence with a heavy transfusion of Federal money."[29] Lisbeth Bamberger, assistant director of the AFL-CIO Social Security Department, voiced labor's support. Governors John Volpe (Mass.), Otto Kerner (Ill.), and John N. Dempsey (Conn.) stated the governors' desire for the staffing funds.

Felix, testifying on behalf of the National Association for Mental Health, declared: "We need the staff before we can operate—and we must begin operating before we can have the funds to finance the necessary staff to make the operation possible."[30] In a final persuasive attempt, he remarked:

> I might say I feel somewhat like Moses in the last chapter of the Book of Deuteronomy when Moses went up on Mount Nebo, and was told to look over the land of Canaan, but the Lord said, "You shall not go over thither." I got closer, but I didn't go there; first we didn't get the staffing provision and then I had to retire.[31]

**The AMA "Opposition."** On its part, the AMA was occupied in the Medicare battle, labeling the Medicare proposal "socialized" medicine.

The organization could not reasonably use the label of "socialized" medicine on every issue nor mobilize its constituency on every health issue before the Eighty-ninth Congress. Since in 1965 Medicare, not staffing, was AMA's key issue, the NIMH leaders took advantage of this fact. They calculated that the general public did not view the staffing of centers as socialized medicine, a point in their favor.[32]

Further, many congressmen, as well as their staffs, were very negative about what appeared in their eyes as AMA's gross economic self-interest surfacing in its opposition to Medicare. Specifically, there existed another factor of promising importance. AMA's opposition to the staffing funds, muted though it was, did not sit well with the members of Congress, especially with those on the Interstate and Foreign Commerce Committee.[33] In presenting the staffing grants, the mental health leadership used timing and the political mood to their advantage. James Z. Appel, M.D., president-elect of AMA, testified:

> The funds for staffing, however, should remain the sole responsibility of the local community. There does not appear to be any justification for Federal participation in financing this type of expense, nor is it likely to phase out as stated in the bill, once the Federal Government has assumed this responsibility.[34]

When Appel's associate, Dr. Robert C. Long, a member of the Board of Trustees, attempted to reinforce the AMA position, the committee members trapped him. Representative Farnsley, a former political scientist, described the lack of funds in poor local communities, in poor states, and in poor counties, plus the lack of sufficient tax bases. Representative Tim Lee Carter, a physician himself and from Appalachia in Kentucky, strongly supported Farnsley. Long retracted:

> *Dr. Long.* Mr. Chairman, I am sorry to be so slow. I must apologize to my own Congressman from my own district for being so slow. Mr. Farnsley, it finally came through my thick head what you are talking about. It is obvious under the terms of your question, where there is a need, if it cannot be met in one manner, it must be met in another manner. And if it cannot be met on the local level or the county or state level, then obviously, if the need can be met on the Federal level, it must be met on the Federal level. Does that answer it?
> *Mr. Farnsley.* That answers it beautifully.[35]

AMA's opposition had indeed been pro forma; it had not mobilized its constituents and had offered weak testimony. In his testimony, which followed Long's, Felix emphasized that the AMA was not monolithic and that many doctors, and certainly the majority of the 15,000 member psychiatrists, supported the staffing provisions.

In 1963, AMA had exerted political pressure on the various committee members and other congressmen; in 1965, all the pressure came from supporters of the bill. Following the hearings, Yolles and Sirotkin worked closely with the committee staff, considering the testimony of the hearings and deciding on the final language of the bill, which was reported unanimously out of committee on April 15, 1965.[36] The report states: "The need for comprehensive community mental health services exists in every area of every state in the Nation." [37] On Tuesday, May 4, the House of Representatives passed H.R. 2985 by a vote of 390 to 0. It authorized federal funds to assist in the initial staffing of community mental health centers.

*Senate Committee on Labor and Public Welfare*

Shortly before June 24, 1965, Senator Hill called his committee into executive session with Yolles in attendance. The committee reported out H.R. 2985 unanimously on June 24, 1965. In general, the Senate report repeats the House report almost verbatim. There were a few deviations in the Senate committee report from the House report:

1. The House didn't go into the matter of leadership of the centers. The Senate committee (after referring to psychologists, psychiatric social workers, and psychiatric nurses) said: "Specifically, overall leadership of the health center program may be carried out by any one of the major mental health professions." [38]

2. The Senate committee did not see the financial role of the federal government as declining. It deleted the following House statement:

No further Federal funds will thereafter be available for the costs of the staffing covered by the prior grants, and the financing of these costs will thereafter be the responsibiiity of the states and localities involved.[35]

The Senate committee seems to have prepared for the contingency of permanent subsidy. The Senate authorized staffing grants to continue through 1972. The House cut them off in 1969.

3. Both the House and Senate bills declared that staffing grants could be made only if the services to be provided were described in the state plan. The Senate, however, deleted the House comment:

The Committee envisions appropriate regulations under this provision which will assure that recommendations of the state mental health authority will be given due weight by both the local community and by the Federal Government in its review of each project application.[40]

Yolles did not want the control of the operating costs to shift to the states by means of the regulations. The state authorities were left with the Senate statement:

State authorities responsible for mental health planning under Title III of the Public Health Service Act can contribute important program perspectives and play a highly significant coordinating role.[41]

4. The Senate report added language calling for the coordination of mental health center programs, not duplication of school guidance and counseling programs under the Elementary and Secondary Education Act of 1965, or housing, antipoverty, and welfare programs.[42]

5. The Senate increased the total money by $51 million.

On June 28, 1965, the U.S. Senate passed H.R. 2985, "Initial Staffing for Mental Health Centers," on a voice vote without debate.

## Senate-House Conference

Hill had added a $186 million "rider" to Section 301 of Public Law 88-164 for grants for training teachers of emotionally disturbed and retarded children. This rider boosted the total bill to one-half billion dollars. On Thursday, July 15, the House rejected the half-billion-dollar, Senate-passed bill and requested a conference with the Senate. In the conference, the House conferees agreed to the Senate's authorization of $224,174,000 for initial staffing over a seven-year period (through 1972). The Senate conferees accepted a rduction of $119 million for additional training and project funds for Title III of Public Law 88-164.

## The Decisive Vote of Congress

On Monday, July 26, 1965, the Senate approved the conference report on a voice vote. In the House, Congressman William Springer, who had opposed the staffing provision in 1963, spoke in support of the conference bill:

At that time (1963) it was suggested that the Federal Government assist in the initial staffing of these facilities. This was not done at that time. Now that the program is underway and the very real problems begin to emerge, it becomes clear that in the case of community mental health centers, some staffing assistance is justified and necessary.[43]

Springer called for a roll call vote. On July 27, 1965, the House adopted the conference report by a unanimous record vote, with 414 yeas, 0 nays, and 19 not voting.

On August 4, President Johnson signed the Community Mental Health Centers Act Amendments of 1965 into Public Law 88-105. He expressed his view that H.R. 2985 was a new legislative landmark "expressing America's broadening concern for the health of all its citizens." He remarked:

The 88th Congress took a giant step forward by making it possible for local communities to secure Federal assistance in constructing mental health centers, and now it is time for another major advance. Now it is time to take more of our mentally ill out of the asylums, and bring them and keep them and care for them close to their homes, in their own familiar surroundings, and in their own communities.

And this legislation really gives us a very new, important tool to use in advancing this concept, by helping the communities staff their own local mental health centers.

This measure and all the others in their field are going to live as a monument to a good many people, and I want to particularly point out Secretary Celebrezze, who is leaving in a short time to go to the court. They also stand as tribute to the *specialized* legislative leadership of skilled craftsmen in the Congress, men such as Lister Hill of Alabama and Oren Harris, Congressman Fogarty.[44]

### The Regulations

The regulations adhered to the basic regulations established from Public Law 88-164.[45] The additional regulation did not specify "professional and technical personnel" in the current categories of mental professions. The language was designed to make provision for inservice and related training. Section 504.305(a)(7) allowed mental health personnel in private practice to treat persons receiving services under the program.

The National Mental Health Advisory Council met on November 14, 1965, to approve unanimously the proposed staffing regulations for community mental health centers. (Public Law 88-105 did not require approval of the regulations by the Federal Hospital Council, thus avoiding another battle with the Hill-Burton interests.) The council expressed its conviction that there should be flexibility in the interpretation of the regulations so that technical and professional staff might be as broadly based as possible.[46] The council encouraged local commitment with respect to planning and resources. The council members' desire to ensure flexibility and innovation reflected concern they had expressed the previous March. At that time, the members were disturbed at the lack of clarity in the definition of the centers' scope, which ranged from a rigid interpretation to one so broad that the mental health center looked every bit like a community social welfare program.[47] The administrative phase and problems had begun even prior to the publication of the regulations on March 1, 1966. Again, as with the centers' construction provisions, the regulations became effective on the date of publication. The *Federal Register's* notice of proposed rule making, public rule-making procedures, and delay of effective date were once again omitted as unnecessary.

### The Meaning of Public Law 89-105

The Community Mental Health Centers Act, Public Law 88-164, was the first federal statement of a "national intent" for care of the mentally ill. The language of the law is as close to a public mandate as has ever been promulgated. However, it leaves to the states and communities the responsibility for the design and the provision of the required services.

Public Law 89-105 was also a landmark piece of legislation. As far as mental health in this country is concerned, it was the turning point. The national policy of care for the mentally ill in their communities rather than in isolation from others is clearly articulated. The administration of the act and subsequent programs can be measured now and in the future at least in terms of their consistency with this national policy.

The passage of Public Law 89-105 resulted in the accomplishment of three objectives:

1. The prestige and power of the president and congressional health leaders increased.

2. The mental health organizations could realistically expect an acceleration of their community programs.

3. The NIMH had not simply enlarged its programmatic scope but also garnered constituencies in local communities in the United States.

Public Law 89-105 was an innovative social policy. The NIMH staffing grant program was nonincremental:

1. The scale and locus of the financing in the federal government changed the scope of community programs from a few random experiments to planned programs destined for all communities.

2. In contrast to most Public Health Service grants, which were tied to the authority of state officials, the staffing grants were in the control of

the NIMH officials, a factor that reinforced the hierarchy in the mental health oligopoly.

3. The staffing grants could be directed more rapidly to the poor because they were project grants subject to the discretion of federal leaders sympathetic to the poor. By November 1965, the National Advisory Mental Health Council requested Yolles, now NIMH director, to explore the mental health tie-in with both the Appalachia and poverty programs.

In 1965 both federal and state officials settled for a bifurcated program: construction grants on the basis of Hill-Burton and staffing grants on a project basis. The states could have insisted that the program be based totally on state formula grants, or the federal government could have demanded complete administrative control. Neither alternative result was acceptable to the political actors. The costs were too high for either the federal or state officials to achieve complete control of the community mental health program. The federally oriented actors could not challenge the construction formula without losing the support of the state authorities. The state-oriented actors were in no position to challenge the staffing grant provisions which did not exclude but financially enhanced their community programs. Although a "political sop," [48] the Hospital Improvement Program and the Hospital Staff Development Program grant funds did provide minimal resources to the state mental hospitals. Although these grants insured the states' endorsement of the staffing grants, their regulations and standards brought the state hospitals more under the control of NIMH. And the Eighty-ninth Congress was pursuing social programs that tended to by-pass state control.

The political decision to implement a national community mental health program meets the Pareto criterion: "State A is declared better than State B if someone is better off in State A and no one is worse off." [49] State A is the provision of federal resources in order to provide the patient population two alternative and interlocking types of care, in the community and in the state hospital, without the deprivation of current state funds for the patients in state hospitals. Perhaps the ultimate effect of that decision would depend on the federal-state-local cooperative incremental adjustments in the administration of the program. The decision itself to depart from warehousing to community-oriented mental health programs was the result of a succession of strategies of a centralized decision-making process in which key actors stuck to an agenda from 1946 to 1966.

## The Resultant Challenge

The success of the legislation would largely depend upon the quality of the administration of the centers program in its implementation stage. Even when the national goal of the Community Mental Health Centers

Program was stated and accepted, and when the machinery was set up to achieve it, a long-term functional policy might not result.

Predictably, the legislative package itself had inherent risks and contradictions as well as advantages and consistency. The obvious risk was the implicit assumption that the leaders who championed the passage of the program would continue to manage and obtain support for it, most particularly within the NIMH and in the communities where the centers would provide services. There was no guarantee that key leaders would remain. Within four years, Felix, Ewalt, Atwell, Fogarty, and Hill were either no longer actively involved or present. The growth of NIMH would force Yolles to delegate much of the execution of the program to persons who might or might not have had the flexibility of the formulators.

If there was no guarantee of continuity of leadership in the execution of the program, the assumption that administrative skill in local communities were sufficient to implement a comprehensive care program requiring multiple sources of funding was open to question. This was not a critical consideration to the oligopoly between 1963 and 1965. The centers program could be viewed as providing the opportunity to develop new leaders and skilled administrators. The danger was that the developmental stage might take too long in the 1960s, when both the public and its representatives desired dramatic results. Popular and congressional support could erode.

A second risk was the joining of the medical services—inpatient, outpatient, emergency, and partial hospitalization services—with the public health services—consultation and education. One goal of the program was to bring the care of the mentally ill into the mainstream of medicine. The twofold programmatic emphasis of the program, however, placed the care of the mentally ill into two mainstreams: medicine and the public health sector. The collaborative functional arrangements among the providers of both types of services would require reeducation for many and surrender of professional insularity for all—a Herculean task. There was the need for many agencies to coordinate their separate programs. Such coordination would require a great deal of compromise and cooperation.

A complication to an already tense alignment of services was the fact that the fiscal reimbursement sources of medicine—public and private insurance and grant programs—excluded the reimbursement of nonphysician providers. In any case, the potential advantage of the conjoining of mental health with public health services was to induce change in the care system. To extend access to mental care without changing the system would incur higher prices for everybody, as the Medicare and Medicaid programs were clearly to demonstrate for the total medical care system. The Community Mental Health Centers Act was an initial attempt to better organize the medical mental health services. Emphasis on nonphysician personnel, preventive medicine, and treatment at home were characteristics of the change in the system. The increased utilization of nonphysicians within the mental health sector placed that subsystem in conflict with the more rigid and reactive medical subsystem of the total human services system. The conflict between these subsystems and tension within the mental health system would call into question the meaning of mental health care in the decade of the 1970s.

Financially, the decision to fund the centers program on a decremental matching basis involved a risk and an advantage. The federal categorical proportion of a center's funding would decrease each year and necessitate funds from other sources to cover the cost for services rendered. One reason for the creation of the program was insufficient local funds for mental health services. This implies that the local community was an unlikely source for new funds. Private insurance was slowly expanding coverage for the treatment of the mentally ill. The process was too slow to offset the decreasing federal categorical grants, although the political actors did not seem to recognize this in the period between 1963 and 1965. Without rapidly increasing funds from other sources, a center would be forced to cut back services and perhaps would go bankrupt. Bankruptcy, then, was a serious risk. There was no guarantee that the federal policy-makers could save centers through new congressional appropriations.

The advantage of the decremental matching would be its potential to create an organized demand for a longer federal subsidy, as the mental health leaders expected, or to occasion the popular demand for increased medical and social insurance through federal or federal-state or private intermediaries, which Wilbur Cohen desired. In 1965 there was an indication that federal participation was the direction. On a noncategorical basis, federal participation was being increased through the relaxation of regulatory restrictions on the utilization of federal funds from Social Security to pay for the cost of treatment of mental illness. It could be foreseen that a cutback on mental health services locally delivered would fuel the anger of local recipients as well as of locally organized boards. They, in turn, would pressure their representatives for a fiscal answer to their problem. If the representatives were not predisposed to the continuation of categorical funding, what would they offer as an adequate substitute? Some type of medical and social funds, federally provided, was a likely candidate. The stage was set either for some type of fiscal guarantee to the citizens of mental health care or else for the clear decision to deny that guarantee. It was unlikely that elected officials would explicitly deny fiscal resources to a population accustomed to financial assistance in obtaining access to a basic human service.

# Notes

1. Memorandum from Robert Atwell to Sirotkin, Administrative Confidential. NIMH Files.

2. Ibid., p. 2.

3. Ibid., p. 6.

4. Interview with Philip Sirotkin, 21 April 1972.

5. Interview with Mr. Mike Gorman, 24 March 1972.

6. Interview with Dr. Stanley Yolles, 23 March 1972.

7. Interview with Wilbur Cohen, 14 June 1972.

8. Lyndon Baines Johnson, "Presidential Policy Paper No. 2—The Nation's Problems of Health, November 1, 1964," *No. 755 Public Papers of the President, Lyndon B. Johnson 1963-64, Vol. II.* (Washington: U.S. Government Printing Office, 1965), p. 564.

9. Sirotkin.

10. Interview with Dr. Jack Ewalt, 12 March 1972.

11. To Henry Foley from Wilbur J. Cohen, 1 April 1975.

12. Cohen.

13. To Stanley Yolles, M.D., from V. Terrell Davis, M.D., 13 January 1965, published by National Association of State Mental Health Program Directors.

14. Yolles.

15. On March 3, 1965, Dr. David Vail (Minn.) sent a telegram to Dr. Isadore Tuerk stating: "Comprehensive Centers Program ill-Conceived: I do not support H.R. 2985" (NASMHD Files).

16. From Dr. William E. Schumacher, to Dr. Stanley Yolles, 1 March 1965 (NASMHD Files).

17. Interview with Walter Barton, 16 March 1972.

18. Lyndon Baines Johnson, "1965 Health Message to Eighty-Ninth Congress.

19. Sirotkin.

20. James Menger, interview, 7 June 1972; Robert Barclay, interview, 13 June 1972.

21. Mrs. Winthrop Rockefeller, quoted by Willard Clopton, "Dollar Aid Urged for Mental Program," *The Washington Post,* 21 February 1965.

22. Dr. Donovan F. Ward quoted in article, "Senator Hill Accuses AMA of Opposing Mental Health Aid," *New York Times,* 20 February 1965.

23. Drawn from testimony of Addison M. Duval, M.D., on behalf of APA in *Hearings* Before the Committee on Interstate and Foreign Commerce, House of Representatives, 89th Congress, 1st Session, on H.R. 2985, 2, 3, 4, and 5 March 1965, p. 205.

24. *New York Times.*
25. Duval.
26. *Hearings,* p. 52.
27. Ibid., pp. 58-59.
28. Isadore Tuerk, M.D., Statement on H.R. 2985 on March 5, 1965, in cited hearings, reproduced by the National Association State Mental Health Program Directors, p. 2.
29. Ibid., p. 6.
30. Ibid., p. 245.
31. Ibid., p. 245.
32. Sirotkin.
33. Menger.
34. Statement of James Z. Appel, M.D., president-elect AMA, in *Hearings,* p. 225.
35. Ibid., pp. 227-28.
36. Sirotkin.
37. House Report No. 248, 89th Congress, 1st Session, p. 7.
38. Senate Report No. 366, Calendar No. 355, 89th Congress, 1st Session, p. 4.
39. House Report No. 248, 89th Congress, 1st Session, p. 6.
40. Ibid., p. 8.
41. Senate Report, p. 6.
42. Ibid., p. 7.
43. *Congressional Record,* 27 July 1965, p. 18430.
44. Emphasis added. Lyndon Baines Johnson, "401. Remarks at the Signing of the Community Mental Health Centers Act Amendments of 1965, August 4, 1965," *Public Papers of the Presidents, Lyndon B. Johnson, 1965, Vol. II.* (Washington: U.S. Government Printing Office, 1966).
45. *Federal Register,* 1 March 1966, p. 3247, Section 54.303(a).
46. Minutes of the National Advisory Mental Health Council, 14 November 1965, p. 3.
47. Minutes of the National Advisory Mental Health Council, 22-24 March 1965.
48. Interview with Robert Atwell, 26 January 1972.
49. Richard Zeckhauser and Elmer Schaefer, "Public Policy and Normative Economic Theory, in *The Study of Policy Formation,* Raymond A. Bauer and Kenneth J. Gergen, eds. (New York: The Free Press, 1968), p. 43.

## Bibliography

*Books*

Connery, Robert H. *The Politics of Mental Health.* New York: Columbia University Press, 1968.

McConnel, Grant. *The Modern Presidency*. New York: St. Martin's Press, 1967.

Simon, Herbert A. *Models of Man*. New York: John Wiley, 1957.


*Articles, Letters, and Memoranda*

"Senator Hill Accuses AMA of Opposing Mental Health Aid," *New York Times,* 20 February 1965.

Clopton, Willard. "Dollar Aid Urged for Mental Program." *The Washington Post,* 21 February 1965.

Ozarin, Lucy D. "New Directions in Community Mental Health Programs." *American Journal of Orthopsychiatry* 35 (1965).

Ozarin, Lucy D. and Alan I. Levenson. "Community Mental Health Programs." *Public Health Reports,* November 1967.

Yolles, Stanley F. "Community Mental Health Services: The View From 1967." *American Journal of Psychiatry* 124, no. 4 (October 1967), Supplement.

Richard Zeckhauser and Elmer Schaefer. "Public Policy and Normative Economic Theory," in *The Study of Policy Formation,* Raymond A. Bauer and Kenneth J. Gergen, eds. New York: The Free Press, 1968.

From Wilbur J. Cohen to Henry A. Foley, 1 April 1975.

From Dr. William E. Schumacher, to Dr. Stanley Yolles, 1 March 1965, NASMHD Files.

From V. Terrell Davis, M.D., to Stanley Yolles, M.D., dated 13 January 1965, published by National Association State Mental Health Program Directors.

On March 3, 1965, Dr. David Vail (Minn.) sent a telegram to Dr. Isadore Tuerk stating: "Comprehensive Centers Program ill-conceived: I do not support H.R. 2985" (NASMHD Files).

Isadore Tuerk, M.D., Statement on H.R. 2985, 5 March 1965, reproduced by the National Association State Mental Health Program Directors.

"Amended Initial Staffing Bill Passes Senate." News Letter from National Association State Mental Health Program Directors, 28 June 1965.

From Robert Atwell to Sirotkin, Administrative Confidential.

Minutes of the National Advisory Mental Health Council, 14 November 1965.

Minutes of the National Advisory Mental Health Council, 22-24 March 1965.


*Addresses*

Lyndon Baines Johnson. "Presidential Policy Paper No. 2—The Nation's Problems of Health, 1 November 1964." *No. 755 Public Papers of the*

*President, Lyndon B. Johnson, 1963-64, Vol. II*. Washington: U.S. Government Printing Office, 1965.

Lyndon Baines Johnson. "1965 Health Message to Eighty-Ninth Congress."

Emphasis added. Lyndon Baines Johnson. "401. Remarks at the Signing of the Community Mental Health Centers Act Amendments of 1965, August 4, 1965." *Public Papers of the Presidents, Lyndon B. Johnson, 1965, Vol. II*. Washington: U.S. Government Printing Office, 1966.


*Public Documents*

*Congressional Record,* 26 July 1965.

*Congressional Record,* 27 July 1965.

Testimony of Addison M. Duval, M.D., on behalf of APA in *Hearings Before The Committee on Interstate and Foreign Commerce, House of Representatives, 89th Congress, 1st Session on H.R. 2985, March 2, 3, 4, and 5, 1965.*

House Report No. 248, 89th Congress, 1st Session.

House Report No. 248, 89th Congress, 1st Session.

Senate Report No. 366, Calendar No. 355, 89th Congress, 1st Session.

*Federal Register,* 1 March 1966, p. 3247, Section 54.303(a).

U.S. Department of HEW, PHS. *Guidelines for State Plans to be Submitted Under the Community Mental Health Centers Act of 1963.* Washington, D.C.: U.S. Government Printing Office, 1965.


*Interviews*

All previous interviews and that of

Mr. Douglas Cater, January 1973.

Mr. Harry Schnibbe, January-March 1972.

Dr. Philip Sirotkin, 21 April 1972.

# 6

## Epilogue: 1965 to 1975

The mental health leaders in Washington who wrote into law the Community Mental Health Centers Act of 1963 and worked their political magic to implement it bear a remarkable resemblance to the Prospero of Shakespeare's *The Tempest*. Like him they were protagonists in a social drama; like him they brought about a spirit of accommodation nationally between the two opposing spirits of idealism and indifference; like him they united two political houses in a common, humanitarian cause: adequate care and treatment for America's mentally ill.

An evaluation of the mental health program in 1973 indicates that (1) there is a continuity and expansion of leadership in mental health services; (2) there is a fixity to the program, despite minor changes; (3) the issue of mental health is no further from the American public than the nearest television screen; (4) the social and medical disciplines continue to concentrate on the mental health problem, and (5) Congress still maintains categorical funding of viable programs.

In short, the 1963 Community Mental Health Centers Act is the archetype for the continuing communality of interest in national mental health legislation. A detailed chronological review of the extent and availability of national mental health services and of quantitative political changes in subsequent legislation amply demonstrates that, even with adjustments, the act has proved workable.

The Community Mental Health Centers Act of 1963 instituted federal grants to communities for the construction of mental health centers. An amendment to the act in 1965 provided federal funds to underwrite the cost of professional and technical personnel servicing the community centers. There was a guaranteed expansion of the overall federal program, with support for individual centers over a fifty-one-month period.

In April 1967, Wilbur Cohen testified for the Department of Health, Education, and Welfare, before the Public Health Subcommittee of the House Committee on Interstate and Foreign Commerce on the extension of the original community mental health centers legislation:

Mr. Chairman, to achieve the goal of making essential community mental health services available to as many people in our country as soon as possible, continued Federal concern and support is essential.

Our goal is to provide these services in every part of our Nation; but our enthusiasm is tempered with realism.[1]

His testimony continued:

The ideal cannot be faulted, and we will not be satisfied until the entire American community is served. . . . We have made only a modest start in meeting the mental health needs of the American people; the great bulk of our population remains to be served through the 2,000 centers planned by 1980.[2]

A report submitted by Senator Lister Hill for the Committee on Labor and Public Welfare on the Mental Health Amendments of 1967 reads:

Our goal for complete coverage is 2,000 centers, but we will fund a total of only 286 community mental health centers by the end of this year.

The emphasis of the 1963 legislation and the 1965 amendments is the provision of comprehensive mental health services throughout the United States. In some communities new construction is required. In other communities only the impetus of matching funds for initial staffing is needed to provide for comprehensive services.[3]

In 1968 the act was expanded. In addition to federal funds for construction and staffing of community mental health centers, there was the provision of services for alcoholics and narcotic addicts. Under the amendments, states could use a portion of their allotment for administration. In 1970 amendments in Public Law 91-212 were generous. They authorized continuance of previously legislated programs and also a new program for specialized services for children. Notably, staffing grants were extended from fifty-one months to eight years. Further, funds were authorized for centers in urban and rural poverty areas on a preferential higher basis. Continued congressional support of the community mental health centers might be measured by the fact that in 1972 they added a further amendment that required centers to provide services for drug addicts or users wherever necessary and feasible.

The primary factors in this expansion are the development of a CMHC interest group and the pragmatic style of the mental health leaders. Directors of federally funded centers formed themselves into the National Council of Community Mental Health Centers. The council quickly became an effective lobby; its primary purpose was to guarantee the continuation and expansion of the centers program. It worked in tandem with other interest groups in the mental health oligopoly, especially NIMH, the

State and Territorial Mental Health Program Directors, and the National Association for Mental Health.

Throughout the period from 1965 to 1970, Dr. Stanley Yolles, the NIMH director, and Dr. Phillip Sirotkin, an associate director, encouraged the development of the council of centers. When Dr. Bertram S. Brown succeeded Yolles in 1970, the council became even more aggressive in pressuring the Congress, the executive branch, and the NIMH itself. The council's most recent successful lobbying activity resulted in Congress mandating a program expansion despite the Office of Management and Budget's decision to phase out the centers program. The NIMH leaders' strategy was to forego the temptation to extol the leaders of the past at the expense of those of the present and to support new executive and legislative leaders without comparing their performance to Fogarty's and Hill's. NIMH staff educated new people in key positions in the executive branch to the problems of mental illness and to the commitments previously made by the federal government to the mentally ill. The impressive growth of the centers program indicates they were successful.

From 1965 to July 1974, the NIMH received $1014 million to develop community mental health centers. The combination of federal, state, and local resources has created 591 centers, 443 in operation by the end of fiscal 1974 and the balance being planned or under construction. Community mental health centers, serving both urban and rural areas, are located in every state, as well as in the District of Columbia, Guam, and Puerto Rico, and cover about 86 million. Center progress has been most rapid in urban areas, primarily because of the existence of some resources and receptive, health-minded community agencies. In rural areas, NIMH has emphasized the development of services where few had previously existed. When those rural centers presently funded become operational, they will be serving approximately 35 percent of the rural population.

The proponents of the centers act had championed the community center as an alternative to mental institutions. Has the concept proved viable? In 1969, 372,000 persons received care in community mental health centers; in 1972 the figure had grown to 846,336, one-third diagnosed as psychotic. One can imagine what effect this increased case load would have had on the mental hospitals, in the absence of CMHC apparatus. Conversely, the patient populations in mental hospitals has declined dramatically. In Kentucky, for example, public mental hospitals registered a 50 percent reduction in patients between 1966 and 1971.

The number and type of clients served by the CMHCs provide data to evaluate the efficacy of the program. CMHCs served 846,336 clients in 1972; 53 percent came from families with less than $5000 income. Of those served in community centers, 44 percent were under age twenty-five; and 4 percent were sixty-five or older. Three out of four persons were treated in center's outpatient services; 23 percent used inpatient care; 4 percent were partially hospitalized.

The data seem to indicate that, both in volume of clientele and various modalities of treatment, the CMHCs are a viable concept. Although the CMHC principle is less than perfect, of greater importance is the number of Americans using the centers for critical service. That volume surpasses the population projected by the mental health leaders in their creation of a national mental health care system. The centers act has worked over the past ten years. The work is not finished if one uses as an index the number of emotionally and mentally disturbed finding rehabilitation in CMHCs, and the number not treated in any health care system. The program was never intended to be a demonstration program but, rather, a service program designed to make comprehensive mental health care available to all citizens who need such care. That citizens are in need is a stark reality.[4]

In 1974, 6 million Americans have sought psychiatric help; many others in need will not. Addicts, children, aged, veterans, and the increasing number of divorced persons require community-based services. There are an estimated half million narcotic addicts. Approximately 5 million persons have intermittently used oral amphetamines without medical prescriptions. Also, an estimated 2 million persons take barbiturates regularly without medical need.

A conservative calculation based on past surveys indicate that 2 or 3 percent of the school children are in need of psychiatric care. Other estimates have ranged from 7 to 12 percent. By using a conservative population projection in 1975, minimally (2 percent in need) 1.5 million children will require mental health services. Assuming a 7 percent estimate of needs, over 5 million children will need help.

At least 3 million older persons (15 percent of the over-65 population) require mental health services.

The number and rate of enlistees and draftees rejected for military service due to psychiatric disorders serve as indicators of mental health problems among young male adults. The medical rejection rate for mental disorders in 1971 was 37.8 per 1000 registrants examined and 12.9 per 1000 enlistees examined. In addition, the psychological and social problems of many Vietnam veterans are manifested in emotional disturbance after discharge from service. Through CMHCs, the self-help groups, storefront clinics, and other supporting systems in local communities can sustain these men in their return to civilian life.

The rates of mental illness treated in state and county mental hospitals, outpatient psychiatric facilities, and general hospital inpatient psychiatric units indicate that between 12 and 16 percent of the 8 million currently divorced and separated persons receive mental health care services each year; more could almost certainly make good use of them.

Despite the extensive documentation of the utilization and need for psychiatric care, the federal reaction to the mentally ill in the early seventies has been disjointed and confusing. The Nixon administration proposed the phasing out of the categorical funding of the Community Mental Health Center Program because the program had been so successful and national health insurance with mental health coverage (which has not been legislated) could substitute for federal categorical support. In pursuit of this objective HEW's Secretary Casper W. Weinberger went so far as to interpret congressional intent by declaring that the program had been intended to be a demonstration project.

Federal support for developing community mental health centers should be seen both for what it is and for what it was originally intended to be—a demonstration project that helped set in motion a major new trend.

It never was intended to be a categorical permanent aid program, and it should not be transformed into one simply because it already exists.[5]

In the fall of 1973 the Senate Health Appropriations Subcommittee reiterated the original intent of Congress and appropriated more funds for the program.

This program was never intended to be a demonstration program—but rather a service program designed to make comprehensive mental health care available to all citizens who need such care. The committee has also included funds to accelerate the establishment of community mental health centers. The committee concurs with the House in rejecting the Administration's proposal to phase out the mental health centers program.[6]

Prior to this legislative action and Weinberger's San Francisco statement, Judge Gerhard Gesell, U.S. District Court for the District of Columbia, declared in August 1973:

The Act was never viewed by Congress as a demonstration program to get communities to follow the examples of others and start their own centers, but rather a national effort to redress the present wholly inadequate measures being taken to meet increasing mental health treatment needs.[7]

The judge ordered the administration to spend the funds appropriated for the centers by the Congress but impounded by President Nixon.

The fall of 1973 could well be described as a "Tempest" of reaction. On the one side, the Congress, the courts, and mental health interest groups defended the principle that there should be federal, state, and private support of community mental health centers. On the other side, the administration attempted, by impounding 1973 federal funds that Congress had appropriated for the centers, to abandon the program. In the process the momentum to establish a network of mental health care settings accessible to all in need seemed to have been derailed. However, the conflict over the program may have resulted in a clearer recognition that both universal entitlement to mental health care coverage and the availability of comprehensive mental health care in community care settings remain critical items.

To continue the development of community mental health care programs, Congress extended the CMHC program for one year by the Health Programs Extension Act of 1973 (P.L. 93-245). The Nixon administration opposed the extension of the community mental health centers legislation, because it argued that the program had proven itself as a demonstration and should now be absorbed by the regular health service delivery system and that it was inequitable to provide federal support for services to only part of the population. The act expired on June 30, 1974. The CMHC program continued on the basis of the Labor-HEW Appropriation Bill for fiscal 1975, which included funds for commitments to complete the eight-year funding of existing centers.

1974 was the year in which Americans had to adjust to a roller-coaster economy of speeding inflation and crashing recession and at the same time absorb the spectacle of leaders of the Nixon administration busy erasing tapes, defending themselves in court, preparing for a full impeachment, resigning, and finally a change in the presidency. Despite the confusion of the period, members of Congress and of the mental health constituencies and the NIMH collaborated to develop a new CMHC act. The formal legislative process follows; the total political processes surrounding this legislation have not yet run their course and consequently are neither analyzed nor described at this time.

**The House**

After hearings were held on February 14, 15, 19, 20, 21 and 22, 1974, the Subcommittee on Public Health and Environment introduced H.R. 14214 as a clean bill (cosponsored by all members of the subcommittee) and unanimously ordered it reported by voice vote on March 19, 1974. The bill covered the authorization for community health centers, migrant health centers, family planning services, health revenue sharing programs, as well as community mental health centers.

On June 27, 1974, Representative Harley Staggers (D-W.Va.) submitted to the House the Report of the Committee on Interstate and Foreign Commerce on H.R. 14214. The administration strongly opposed this bill because it would extend the existing program, add new programs and authorities, and otherwise amend the authorities for which the administration proposed either a phase-out, consolidation, or a policy of no new starts or expansion, such as community mental health centers, family planning, migrant health, state comprehensive formula grants, and community health centers. In addition, the administration felt that the authorization levels were excessive. On August 12, 1974, the House passed H.R. 14214. The vote was taken by electronic device and there were: yeas, 359, nays, 12, not voting, 63.

On the same day Secretary Casper W. Weinberger notified Senator Harrison A. Williams, Jr. (D-N.J.), chairman of the Senate Committee on Labor and Public Welfare, that the administration opposed the expansion of the CMHC program and especially the congressional writing of detailed requirements relative to the administration of the CMHC program as well as the other health programs contained in H.R. 14214 and S. 3280.

Also, in August 1974, the General Accounting Office reported to the House Subcommittee on Public Health and Environment that without continued federal assistance a number of existing services, especially outpatient care for low-income groups and consultation and education for all, would probably be curtailed or eliminated at many centers. Alternative financial assistance for these services were not realistically or adequately available to replace the federal categorical funds.

**The Senate**

Hearings were held before the Subcommittee on Health of the Senate Committee on Labor and Public Welfare on April 30 and May 1 and 2, 1974. Senator Kennedy introduced S. 3280 to amend the Public Health Service Act to revive and extend programs of health service delivery and health revenue sharing. Despite the administration's continuing opposition, the Senate Committee on Labor and Public Welfare reported favorably S. 3280 on September 5, 1974. Within five days, the Senate passed H.R. 14212 and requested a conference with the House of Representatives on the legislation. Eight days later (September 18, 1974) the major interest groups circulated their suggested compromise on provisions effecting community mental health centers in H.R. 14212 and S. 3280 to the House and Senate conferees.

On November 26, 1974, the conferees reached agreement on Title II—

Community Mental Health Centers—of the "Health Revenue Sharing and Health Service Act of 1974." Their conviction on the success of the community mental health centers is evident:

(1) community mental health care is the most effective and humane form of care for a majority of mentally ill individuals;

(2) the federally funded community mental health centers have had a major impact on the improvement of mental health care by—

    (A) fostering coordination and cooperation between the various agencies responsible for mental health care, which in turn has resulted in a decrease in overlapping services and more efficient utilization of available resources,

    (B) bringing comprehensive community mental health care to all in need within a specific geographic area regardless of ability to pay, and

    (C) developing a system of care which insures continuity of care for all patients.

(3) that there is a shortage and maldistribution of community mental health resources in the United States.[8]

On December 9, 1974, the Senate accepted the report of the conference by voice vote. The next day the House did likewise, by a vote of 372 to 14.

Congress expanded the services to be offered by CMHCs to include inpatient and outpatient services, follow-up care for residents discharged from mental health facilities, service programs for prevention and treatment of alcoholism and drug abuse (optional), specialized mental health services for children and the elderly, consultation and education services, and assistance to courts and other public agencies. Congress also required that halfway houses be provided for patients discharged from a facility who are certified as mentally ill and are residents of a center's catchment area. Six types of CMHC grant supports were authorized for: CMHC planning, their initial operations, the conversion of existing centers to the new program, consultation and education services, for CMHCs in financial distress, and the development of CMHC facilities.

On December 25, President Ford vetoed H.R. 14214 because, as he stated, "I just cannot approve this legislation because of its effect upon the economy through increased unwarranted Federal spending."[9]

In 1975 this social-political struggle will resume.

# Notes

1. U.S. Congress. Subcommittee on Public Health and Welfare of the Committee on Interstate and Foreign Commerce. House of Representatives. *Hearings on Mental Health Centers Construction Act Extension of 1967,* 90th Congress, 1st Session, 4, 5 April 1967.
2. Ibid.
3. Ibid.
4. *Congressional Record,* 4 October 1973.
5. Secretary Casper W. Weinberger, quoted in the *San Francisco Chronicle,* 5 October 1973.
6. *Congressional Record,* 4 October 1973.
7. Judge Gerhard Gesell, *National Council of Community Mental Health Centers* v. *Weinberger.*
8. 93rd Congress, 2nd Session, Senate/Conference Report No. 93-1311, "Health Revenue Sharing and Health Services Act of 1974," p. 60.
9. President Gerald R. Ford, "Memorandum of Disapproval, December 21, 1974" Office of the White House Press Secretary, 23 December 1974.

**Bibliography**

*Books*

The Center for Study of Law. *The Madness Establishment.* New York: Grossman Publishers, 1974.

*Articles*

*San Francisco Chronicle,* 5 October 1973.

*Public Documents*

*Congressional Record,* 4 October 1973.
U.S. Congress. Subcommittee on Public Health and Welfare of the Committee on Interstate and Foreign Commerce, House of Representatives. *Hearings on Mental Health Centers Construction Act Extension of 1967,* 90th Congress, 1st Session, 4, 5 April 1967.
Subcommittee on Public Health and Environment of the Committee on Interstate and Foreign Commerce, House of Representatives. *Community Mental Health Centers.* 93rd Congress, 1st Session, March, 1973.

# 7

## Analytical Overview

The preceding chapters have described the origins, development, and enactment of the Community Mental Health Centers Act. Interlaced with the description has been a discussion of several models of decision making and political action that helps to order these events from the perspective of political science.

This final chapter highlights some of the more significant moments, those where theory and fact meet and both are rendered more intelligible. It explores the community mental health center movement as a case study in social policy formation. The framework of the analysis is developed around answers to four questions:

1. Why did the federal government become increasingly involved in the delivery of services to the mentally ill?

2. From what organizational contexts and pressures did the decisions emerge?

3. Was this process one of central decision making or partisans bargaining among themselves?

4. What kinds of lobbying, mobilizing, and bargaining arrangements among which players yielded the critical decision that resulted in a national community mental health program?

### The Analytical Framework

Political theorists Robert Dahl and Charles Lindblom suggest that political processes can be described in four forms: hierarchy, polyarchy, price system, and bargaining.

The first, *hierarchy,* is a political process in which leaders exercise a very high degree of unilateral control over nonleaders. It has two distinctive characteristics: "Non-leaders cannot peacefully displace leaders after explicit or implicit voting; and leaders substantially decide when, in what conditions, and with whom consultation takes place." [1]

*Polyarchy* is a constellation of social processes in which nonleaders exercise a relatively high degree of control over leaders. It has two major characteristics: nonleaders can peacefully displace leaders after explicit or nonexplicit voting, and when they so wish, "elected leaders have the last word on policy with nonelected officials." [2]

A *price system,* the third form, is

> a highly differentiated sociopolitical process for controlling the relations between leaders and non-leaders in the economizing process. It simplifies the economizing process primarily by quantification through prices and delegation through decentralization. Its more particular characteristics are free consumer and occupational choices, specific controls to compel entrepreneurs to respond to the consumer and occupational choices expressed, and an elaborate mechanism of manipulated field control through which leaders can organize production by bringing resources holders under hierarchical controls within each enterprise.[3]

*Bargaining* is a form of reciprocal control among leaders. Lindblom terms the process of bargaining over American governmental policy *partisan mutual adjustment.* The participants are executives of agencies, actual and potential legislators, citizens, interest-group leaders, and party leaders. They constantly bargain with each other, both bilaterally and multilaterally, in all possible combinations. The partisan decision-maker is one among a group of decision-makers, who first,

> does not assume that there exists some knowable criteria acceptable to him and all the other decision makers that is sufficient, if applied, to govern adjustments among them [and] therefore does not move toward coordination by a cooperative and deliberate search for and/or application of such criteria or by an appeal for adjudication to those who do search and apply.
>
> A partisan decision maker is therefore one who makes decisions calculated to serve his own goals, not goals presumably shared by all other decision makers with whom he is interdependent, except as is controlled by other partisans or by central supervision.[4]

The partisan decision-maker can be contrasted to the central decision-maker,

> who (a) is in a symmetric control relation with every other member of the set; (b) in every such symmetric control relation is much more powerful than the other, except for the other's control through information and analysis; and (c) explicitly recognizes his task to be arranging the adaptations of decisions one to another, and to some significant degree arranges such adaptations.[5]

No one central decision maker so defined can be identified in the case of the Community Mental Health Centers Act. Several partisans working collaboratively formulated the act.

The process that led to the act is a mix of the four types of political processes, although partisan mutual adjustment is predominant and there are strong traces of hierarchy. The decision-makers who participated in the policy formulation bargained as partisans—but not partisans locked into a process of mutual adjustment. The actual process could be characterized as the oligopolistic form of partisan mutual adjustment, which in its pure form does not include coordination of the partisans. Yet several of the partisans in the passage of the Community Mental Health Centers Act emerged at specific moments as coordinators out of an oligopolistic base of power. A few decision-makers controlled a mental health establishment and the demand from many providers of services. In fact, they had sufficient control to depart from an incremental pattern of decision making about mental health services to a quick major shift in policy about the delivery of mental health services. Rather than proposing marginal changes in the financing and delivery of services, the partisans advocated and obtained major changes in financing and organizing that delivery.

### Oligopolistic Bargaining and the CMHC Case

The processes of hierarchy, polyarchy, and price system are contained often within partisan mutual adjustment. These processes were apparent in the case of the centers act. Hierarchy can be seen in the fact that, within the NIMH, Felix and Yolles exercised a high degree of unilateral control over the staff in the NIMH. Polyarchy was present, because the president and Congress had the last legislative word on policy with non-elected HEW officials, although these officials helped to define the legislative wording on the centers program in terms advantageous to special interests, especially the American Psychiatric Association. The psychiatric elite within the federal health bureaucracy was able to organize the production of mental health services by bringing resource-holders (state and local communities) under hierarchical controls through formula and project grants.

Yet, throughout this story, evidence has been offered that the CMHC policy resulted from a process of decision making by allied partisans. Critical political actors made policy according to a process that necessitated explicit agreements and goals. The Community Mental Health Centers Act did not evolve out of a series of marginal moves and uncoordinated decisions that necessitated only vague agreement on broad goals. Rather, the mental health oligopoly provided a public policy responsive to technical knowledge and congressional sentiment that it had moulded.

The mental health oligopoly had evolved over a period of fifteen years. It can be characterized as a professional lobby acting upon, and most often in concert with, members placed in the federal government. Its membership consisted of the leaders of a federal bureau, the National Institute of Mental Health, leaders of five major interest groups, the American Psychiatric Association, the American Psychological Association, the National Committee Against Mental Illness, the National Association for Mental Health, The National Association of State Mental Health Program Directors, and congressional spokesmen in the Senate Committee on Labor and Public Welfare, the House Committee on Interstate and Foreign Commerce, and the appropriations committees from both the House and Senate.

The development of the oligopoly had major cutting points. World War II and the ever rising admissions and retentions of patients in state mental hospitals had highlighted the need for community psychiatry and for the prevention of mental illness. Psychiatric, congressional, journalistic, and philanthropic leaders emerged to institutionalize their agenda. Ewalt, Felix, Hill, Priest, Fogarty, Gorman, and Lasker stand out as the most noteworthy actors in the nonincremental fiscal growth period of the National Institute of Mental Health. The institute benefited from the nonincremental fiscal approach of these strategists contributing to the tremendous growth of the National Institutes of Health.

The research and training programs of NIMH prospered. However, the original service programs—the Title V project grants—centered on demonstrations and were funded on a low-incremental basis. This was due to the research bias in the institute as well as congressional unwillingness to involve the government in direct mental health services to the total population. Paradoxically, research on drugs, the congressional promotion of the development of chemotherapy, and the production of more psychiatrists by means of NIMH training grants were to make the comprehensive community mental health program technically feasible. Drugs could be used to stabilize individuals and prevent their institutionalization; psychiatrists were available to provide care in the community at a time when there had been a decline in the status of state mental hospital psychiatrists. Yet, the Title V grants did provide the NIMH leaders the means to offer the states economic inducements to follow their advice on what direction the mental health programs should take.

In the pre-1960 period, the NIMH leaders, especially Felix, built up a base of power. Their power was initially unequal to the state commission-ers of mental health, then gradually was equalized through the use of grants that put the states in a situation of partial dependence for fiscal and technical resources, and finally became stronger than other partisans.

From 1955 to 1960, the Joint Commission on Mental Illness and Health and the popular press propaganized the American public on the causes and nature of mental illness, the need for a major switch from the evils of warehousing to community care, and the fiscal needs for federal involvement. The commission also co-opted every major interest group and sold the mental health issue as nonpartisan. The professional psychiatric leaders in the commission and their colleagues in the institute always presented the care of the mentally ill as a nonpartisan issue. This type of strategy has continued into 1975.

During this mobilization period, the Joint Commission recommended the fiscally conflicting proposals of massive federal support of state hospitals and massive federal support of community programs to meet demands of pro and con state hospital partisans. The commission also proposed increased funding for research and training, which satisfied the concerns of universities and medical schools.

By 1960, American concern was focused not on the government's move toward involvement in the health care sector, but rather on the nature of that involvement. Reasonably, the concern for the care of the mentally ill could not be separated from the general public movement for general health care for the aged, the poor, the handicapped, and others. At that time, government elites were debating the scope and objects of direct federal financing of personal health services.

Neither equity nor the informed judgment of the mental health elite argued for an incremental approach in distribution of new benefits to all mentally ill. An incremental approach would have meant only more demonstrations too inadequately funded to have any major impact. The fiscal base for the service programs in NIMH was too small to underwrite national mental health objectives. Incrementalism was politically unacceptable to both presidents who espoused an activist social policy. For example, President Kennedy had a special interest in the mentally retarded and wanted a "bold" national program directed to them and the mentally ill. President Johnson was attempting to create the Great Society with major federal involvement in the health and education sectors. Such presidential intentions coincided with the dual desire of Felix and Yolles to expand the service base of NIMH and its scope of power.

Faced with the political pressure from the White House and the Hill for a nonincremental public policy, the mental health oligopoly operated in a situation of internal bargaining. The slow movement toward comprehensiveness in the delivery of community mental health services had led the mental health leaders to the conclusion that the incremental approach was not enough. They were presented the opportunity to voice their own solution in the President's Task Force on Mental Health.

The fulcrum of power for the design of a national program was with the central staff of the NIMH. The staff, led by Felix and Yolles, created the comprehensive community mental health center, packaged out of the operational, programmatic elements of the Title V project grants drawn from the example of several states' community mental health programs. They marketed the package to the president's task force, and they bargained.

Within the task force, Felix, and especially Yolles, had to concede to the positions of the state-oriented political appointees such as Moynihan. They were also savvy enough to work out the Hospital Improvement Program and Hospital Staff Development Program as mechanisms to buy off political opposition and garner support from state mental health officials. Both programs were, and still are, badly needed. State hospitals would also be allowed to covert to, or become a part of, community mental health center arrangements. Through such bargaining, Felix could provide economic incentives to keep the state officials a part of the NIMH constituency. Further, he could pick up local community constituencies by means of federal grants.

The critical asset that Felix had in the bargaining within the task force was the professional respect that the other members had for him. They judged that what his staff designed and what he presented was scientifically acceptable. There was evidence of beneficial medical and social effects that the program would produce. While data existed to support the feasibility of a nationwide mental health program as Felix proposed it, there were no data to prove that (as later defined in the regulations) the comprehensive approach would be effective. Admittedly, the programmatic elements in combination were not that certain of positive results. In fairness to Felix, to the other members of the task force, and to key leaders outside the task force, it must be noted that none of them considered the centers program as cast in concrete. All assumed that various elements of the program might have to be modified. The actual evolution of the centers legislation contained in the amendments of 1965 through 1972 to the Health Revenue Sharing and Health Services Act of 1974 is indicative that Congress could both understand and support modifications of the program.

One of the key functions of certain members of the president's task force was to keep within the fold the American Medical Association, one of the members of the oligopoly. The AMA had become a member through its activities on the joint commission and through its own Council on Mental Health. It had publicly endorsed community care provided by local physicians. But on the issue of federal involvement with comprehensive community mental health care, because of its political philosophy, the AMA became a partisan in partial opposition to the mental health oligopoly, because it feared more federal control and the "forcing" of doctors into group practice in centers. The AMA concern was justified; CMHCs and other federal health legislation did in fact place the medical sector under increasing government discretion.

Throughout late 1962 and the early part of 1963, Jones and Felix attempted to show the AMA leaders that the CMHC was a movement *away* from socialized medicine and that, even though the federal government would become involved in the reimbursement of physicians, the fee-for-service system would be maintained. The reimbursement issue was critical to the AMA, just as it would be in the Medicare battle and now in the National Health Insurance debate. That issue specifically concerned the nature of federal involvement, not the need for it.

When the AMA perceived the staffing grants as a potential danger to their reimbursement position, the organization opposed the program and occasioned the GOP partisan tactics that forced the congressional allies of the oligopoly to settle for a "bricks-and-mortar" program in 1963. By 1965, the mental health leaders, through the mediation of the American Psychiatric Association, could point out to the AMA leaders that the reimbursement question was no longer an issue. Through the CMHC program, it was argued, the physician could provide care to the blue-collar worker and to the poor, while being compensated in the same manner as he was reimbursed for services rendered to middle-to-upper-class clientele. Current data shows that CMHCs are serving the poor, but it was only the later Medicaid program that made it feasible for some of the poor to pay according to a fee-for-service system. The APA leaders, who of course were also AMA members, obtained the AMA's agreement not to actively oppose the staffing grants. And, in 1965, the Johnson victory did not allow the GOP to adopt partisan tactics again against a historically nonpartisan issue, the care of the mentally ill.

In the legislative stage, the NIMH leaders accepted the separation of the mental retardation programs from the NIMH in order to satisfy the mental retardation interest groups, because of President Kennedy's and Congressman Fogarty's expressed desires, and consequently picked them up as allies for legislative action. Felix, through Cohen, gave up on continuing the mental retardation efforts of the NIMH. He did so to meet the demands of Eunice Shriver and President Kennedy that the National Institute for Child Health and Human Development and the Social Rehabilitation Services have lead responsibility for the research, training, and care of the mentally retarded. Thus, by divesting himself of the mental retardation program, he was able to get more funds directed toward the mentally ill. However, it was years later that the NIMH staff lost what may be termed a holding battle on the mental retardation program.

The key partisans, Kennedy, Hill, Harris, and Felix had to bide their time for a complete program when Congress eliminated staffing as a response to the AMA partisans. AMA finally muted its opposition because the American Psychiatric Association had obtained its support in return for alliance with the AMA on other issues. The Medicare issue also had distracted the AMA.

The notion of centers for the constituents of every congressman was a bargaining device to gain positive congressional reaction. History has shown that many centers are in fact in the districts of those in the committees relevant to NIMH.

On the policy of the community mental health centers, the formal oligopolistic center of power becomes clear when one examines the regulations rested on central decision making within NIMH. If the strategy of the Yolles coalition was, in fact, full (100 percent), long-term federal financing of all community mental health services (and there are hints of such a strategy), it failed precisely because other partisans on the state level required partnership. Had the coalition succeeded, the 1965 CMHC act would be an instance of central decision making. The actors on the federal level would have had full control. They did not. In the formulation of regulations and standards, the NIMH leadership accepted partial state control in the implementation of the program while at the same time delineating the basic criteria of the program the states had to accept.

## The Outcome

The United States partially federalized its mental health care because the mental health oligopoly focused around the National Institute of Mental Health could provide a technocratically feasible and federally controlled program attuned to the political climate. The federal government became involved in the delivery of mental health services for two reasons. It had the fiscal resources and the mental health leaders and the political leaders within the federal government. (The Nixon administration's opposition to the centers legislation from 1969 to 1973 raises the question of what the outcome of this movement would have been had Richard M. Nixon won the closely contested 1960 election.) Both from humanitarian and personal needs, these professional oligopolists sought to erect a program to meet the needs of the mentally ill and to protect their control over research, training, and care. Both objectives did not seem contradictory to them.

What is remarkable is the successful formulation of the program within the HEW bureaucracy, along with its acceptability to the Congress and to the presidents. The pressures of the time and the special abilities of the persons involved offer a partial explanation. The technocratic base for the program existed. The general public would accept a program. Influential persons, such as Eunice Shriver and Mary Lasker, acted as catalysts.

The fuller explanation lies in the fact that they and others were active participants in a network of decision-makers who shared a common general goal. They might fight among themselves over specifics, but they never fought in public. Consequently, they were amenable to coordinating their efforts. This became very evident when the national lobby groups followed Gorman's directions in the legislative process. The critical decision to have a program at all may be ascribed to President Kennedy, in the sense that without his formal leadership, the program would not have been presented to Congress in 1963. The critical decision of the specific nature and need of that program belongs to the members of the mental health oligopoly. They provided both presidents and Congress what, in their best professional judgment, was appropriate for the country and acceptable.

Certain conditions allowed for the formulation and enactment of the Community Mental Health Centers Act. The Washington-based mental health leaders presented their cause as noncontroversial and nonpartisan. These leaders had a federal institutional base from which they developed a psychiatric technology through the control and direction of federal research, training, and demonstration funds. They managed opposition within their oligopoly by bargaining. Effective opposition to their community thrust from outside the oligopoly did not exist. They judged that incrementalism in the federal role in the delivery of mental health services was inappropriate. Their judgments coincided with that of two mandating presidents and a Congress sympathetic to both the philosophy of the program and to federal resources for the program in a favorable period of economic growth. Their easy access to technology, to congressional committees, to the presidents, and to informed interest groups gave them more power than all other mental health leaders. They coordinated their activities, rather than squandered their power through competition. But there is no evidence that they acted in a synoptic fashion as a central decision-maker might. They knew neither all the alternatives to their actions nor the consequences. Their perspective was community psychiatry for all—a quite unspecific ideology. The outcome of their coordinated political activities was a nonincremental shift in public policy.

The Community Mental Health Centers Act was not a marginal shift or a minute increase in an ongoing program. The fiscal increase over two years for community programs alone was significantly high and rapid. The legislation created a new governmental relationship, a triad of federal government, state government, and local community involvement in the delivery of mental health care services.

The incrementalist view might have argued that a marginal change would have been acceptable in 1963 and 1965, and yet such an argument would have been fallacious, because it would have been at odds with a clear, rational discrediting of a rather extensive mental health care system centered in state mental hospitals. The Community Mental Health Centers Act offered an instance in which a major programmatic shift, occurring in a system of evolutionary change, was appropriate to the needs and demands of the body politic. The system of the state mental health hospitals had been given the responsibility for the care of the mentally ill from communities and from families who were quite willing to surrender that responsibility. In contrast, the Community Mental Health Centers Act restored the responsibility for the care to local communities and to families who wanted it or not. The act provided a supportive system designed to assist those communities and families. Paradoxically, it pressured these traditional structures at a time when much of the social policy in this country threatened the breakdown of the local community and family structure. The mental health oligopolists did not face the critical question of what would be the social cost for the community and family themselves when they assumed a greater responsibility for the care of the mentally ill.

The decision-makers in the NIMH, the Bureau of the Budget, the HEW Secretary's Office, the President's Office, Congress, and the lobbies decided that a nonincremental change was necessary for the care of the mentally ill in the United States. Marginal reform for a continuation and buttressing of state mental health hospital systems would have been a totally inappropriate approach, and yet this is what an incremental approach would have argued for. The policy-makers were concerned with building and staffing more centers, with maintaining the mentally ill in the community, reducing the incidence of mental illness, and with adding prevention and consultation techniques. In short, they were concerned with how to provide enough care, and not primarily how to make care better. To the extent they were concerned with the type of desirable mental health care system, they focused on access and continuity of comprehensive services, defined as inpatient, outpatient, partial hospitalization, emergency, consultation, and education services.

This case study suggests that in the area of mental health, national mental health programs depend upon rational calculation and control responsive to the political mechanisms of bureaucratic agencies, congressional bodies, presidential councils, and interest groups. The case of the Community Mental Health Centers Act demonstrates that calculation and control can occur when informed political opinion and those who manage the technocratic base can, in coordination, demand a major shift in policy.

Once that shift has become a federal policy applicable to the whole country, it may be impossible for an administration to negate the policy—a reality the Nixon administration discovered from 1970 to 1974.

It should not go unsaid that critical human enriching elements to the mental health oligopoly have been but hinted at rather than explored. These elements are the personalities, the friendships and hostilities of the members, the changing ambience of their meetings at the Cosmos Club in Washington, the blend of desires and pragmaticism that structured their informed decisions, thus cementing their oligopoly. The future biographies of Gorman, Lasker, Felix and allies mentioned in this case study may provide information about the interpersonal factors that conditioned the bargains of the mental health oligopoly. If so, our notions of policy making in the area of health will be enriched.

# Notes

1. Robert A. Dahl and Charles E. Lindblom, *Politics, Economics and Welfare* (New York: Harper and Brothers, 1953), p. 227.
2. Ibid.
3. Ibid., p. 177.
4. Charles E. Lindblom, *The Intelligence of Democracy* (New York: The Free Press, 1965), p. 29.
5. Ibid., p. 105.

## Bibliography

*Books*

Barton, Harvey H. and Leopold Bellak, eds. *Progress in Community Mental Health.* New York Times & Stratton, 1972.
Bauer, Raymond A., Thiel de Sola Pool, and Lewis Anthony Dexter. *American Business and Public Policy.* New York: Atherton Press, 1968.
Bauer, Raymond A. and Kenneth J. Gergen. *The Study of Policy Formation.* New York: The Free Press, 1971.
Beer, Samuel H. *British Politics in the Collectivist Age.* New York: Vintage Books, 1969.
Dahl, Robert A. and Charles E. Lindblom. *Politics, Economics and Welfare.* New York: Harper and Brothers, 1953.
Downs, Anthony. *Inside Bureaucracy.* Boston: Little Brown and Co., 1967.
Lawrence, Paul R. and Jay W. Lorsch. *Organization and Environment.* Boston: Division of Research, Graduate School of Business Administration, Harvard University, 1967.
Lindblom, Charles E. *The Policy Making Process.* Englewood Cliffs, N.J.: Prentice-Hall, Inc., 1968.
Lindblom, Charles E. *The Intelligence of Democracy.* New York: The Free Press, 1965.
Morris, Peter and Martin Rein. *Dilemmas of Social Reform.* New York: Atherton Press, 1967.
Rourke, Frances E. *Bureaucratic Power in National Politics.* Boston: Little, Brown and Co. 1965.
Sindler, Allan R., ed. *American Political Institutions and Public Policy.* Boston: Little, Brown and Co., 1969.

Stinchcombe, Arthur L. *Construction Social Theories*. New York: Harcourt, Brace and World, Inc., 1968.

Thompson, James D. *Organizations in Action*. New York: McGraw-Hill Book Company, 1967.

Titmuss, Richard M. *Commitment to Welfare*. New York: Pantheon Books, 1968.

Wolfinger, Raymond E. *Readings in American Political Behavior*. Englewood Cliffs, N.J.: Prentice-Hall, Inc., 1966.


*Articles*


Alford, Robert F. "The Political Economy of Health Care: Dynamics Without Change." *Politics and Society,* Winter 1972.

Marmor, Theodore R. and Carol Merney. "The Politicization of Personal Health Services." *Institute for Research on Poverty,* University of Wisconsin, Madison, August 1969.

# Index

# About the Author

**Henry A. Foley** has been Deputy Director and Planning Chief for the Office of Program Development and Analysis and has been Senior Health Economist for the National Institute of Mental Health in Washington, D.C. He also served as the Deputy Director for the Office of Program, Planning and Evaluation for the Alcoholism, Drug Abuse and Mental Health Administration. Prior to his work as a health economist, Dr. Foley had been the Deputy Director of the Community Action Agency in Milwaukee. He earned the Ph.D. and the M.A. in Political Science from Harvard University; the M.S. in Urban Affairs from the University of Wisconsin, Milwaukee; the M.A. in Theology from Marquette University and the B.A. in Philosophy from St. John's College.

Dr. Foley has published and lectured widely on various aspects of mental health planning delivery systems, political and community support and funding. He is currently the Executive Director of the Colorado Department of Social Services, an umbrella-like agency which includes Income Maintenance, Social Services, Medical Assistance, Rehabilitation, Services for the Aging, and Veterans Programs.